BUTTERFLY
TATTOOS

JOHNNY KARP

Butterfly Tattoos
by Johnny Karp

ISBN 978-0-9866426-7-8

Printed in the United States of America

Other Books in the Series

Other titles are in preparation.

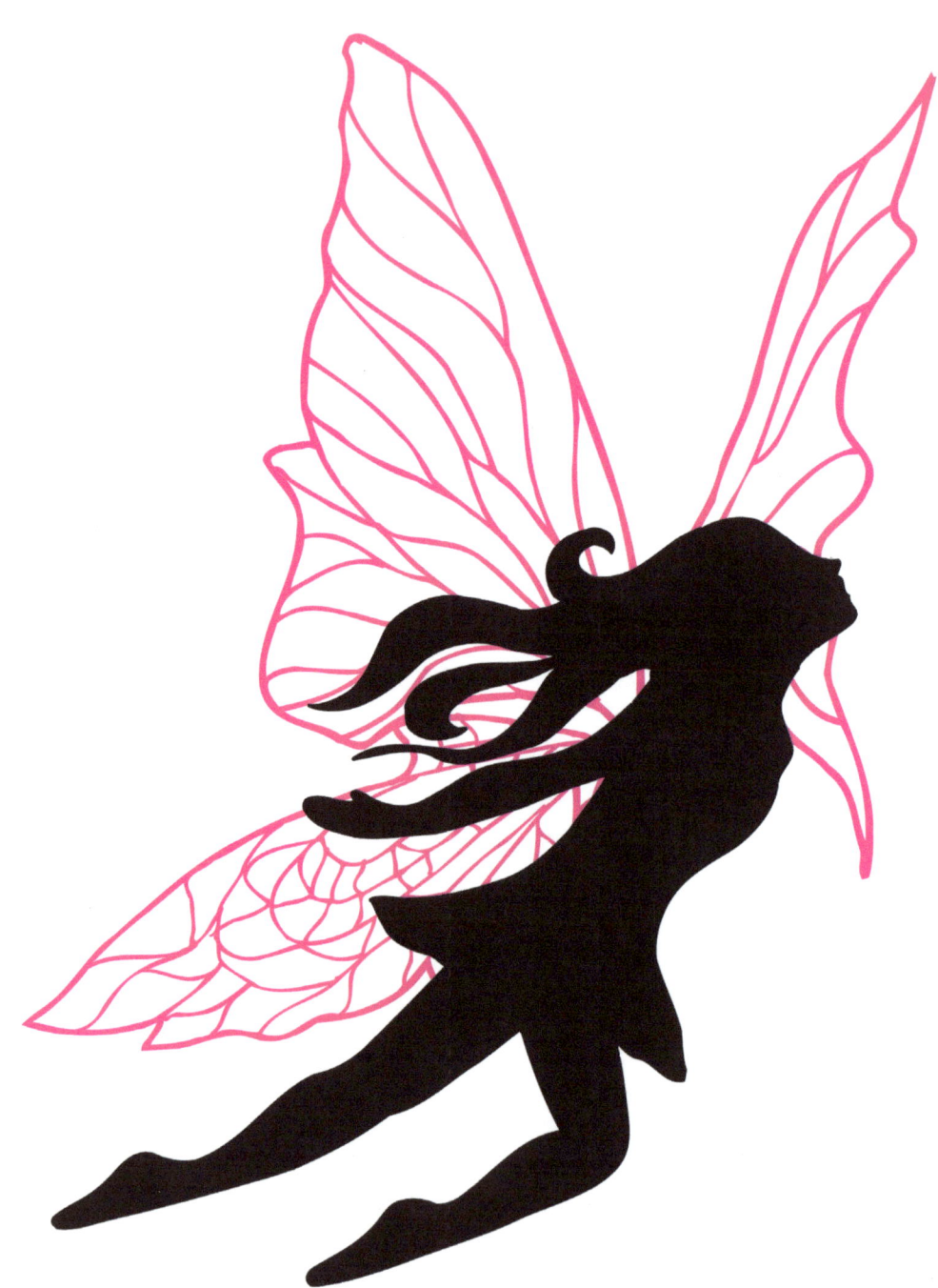

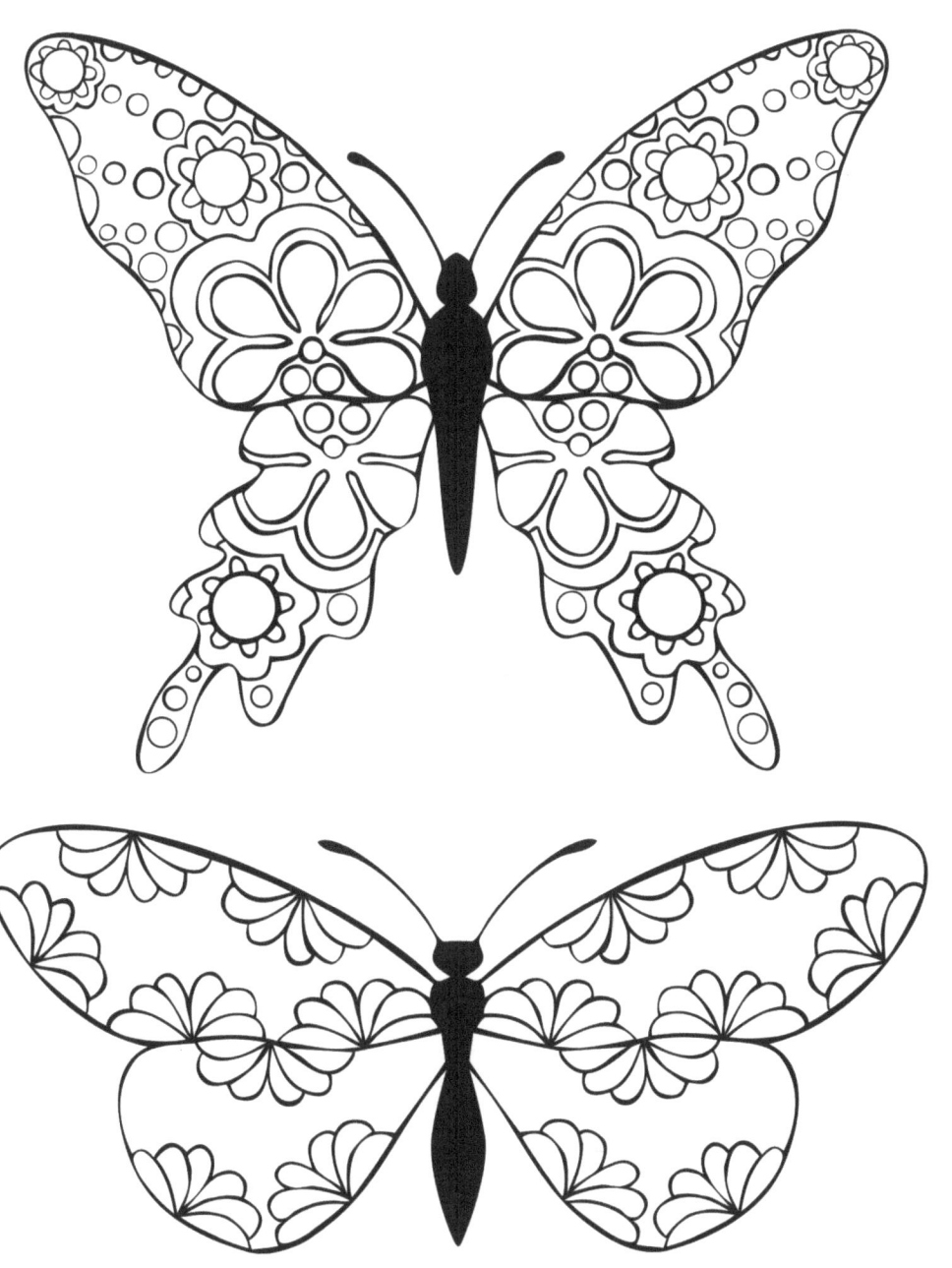

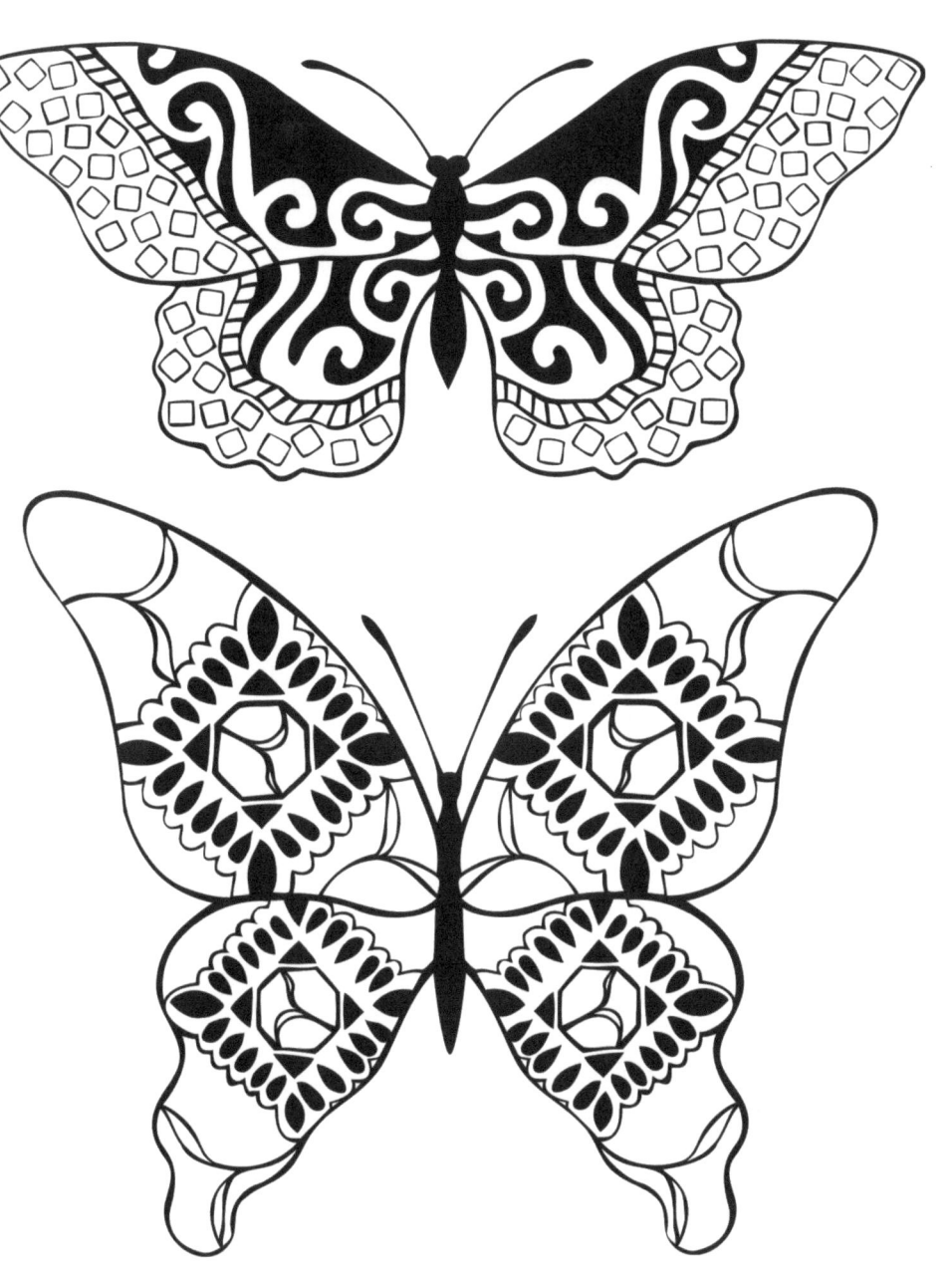

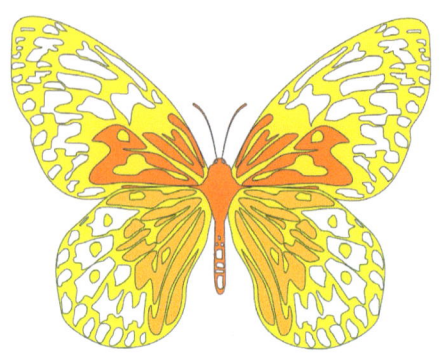
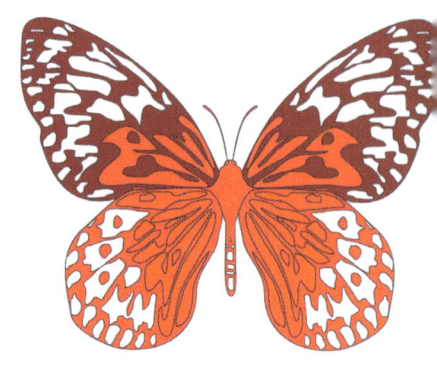
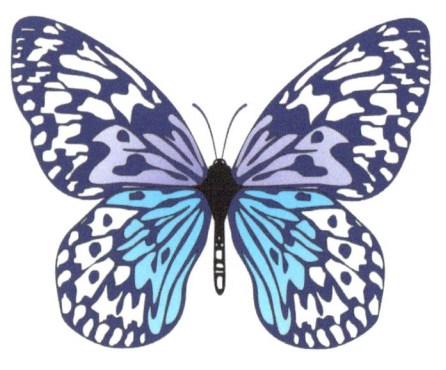
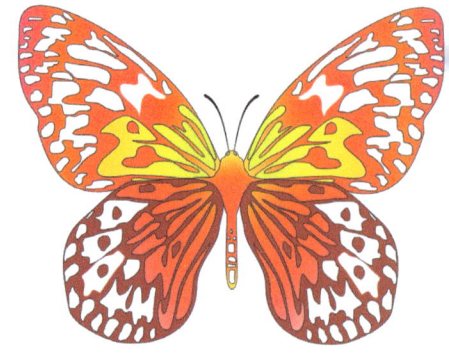
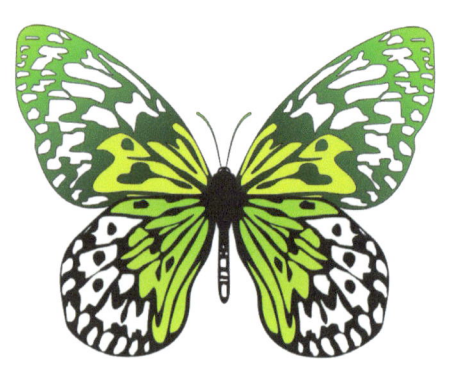
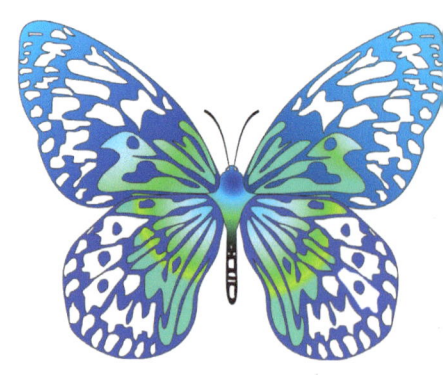

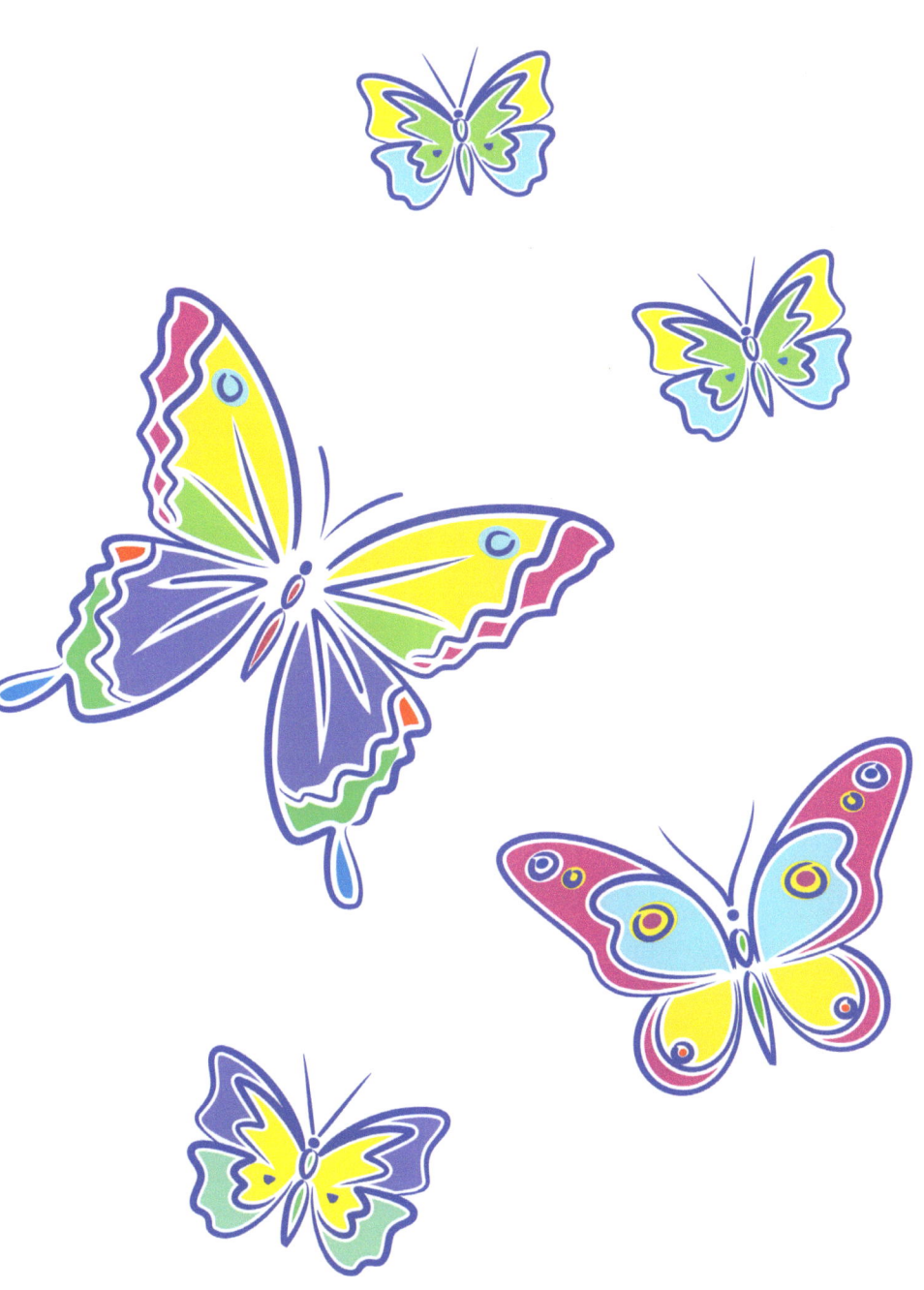

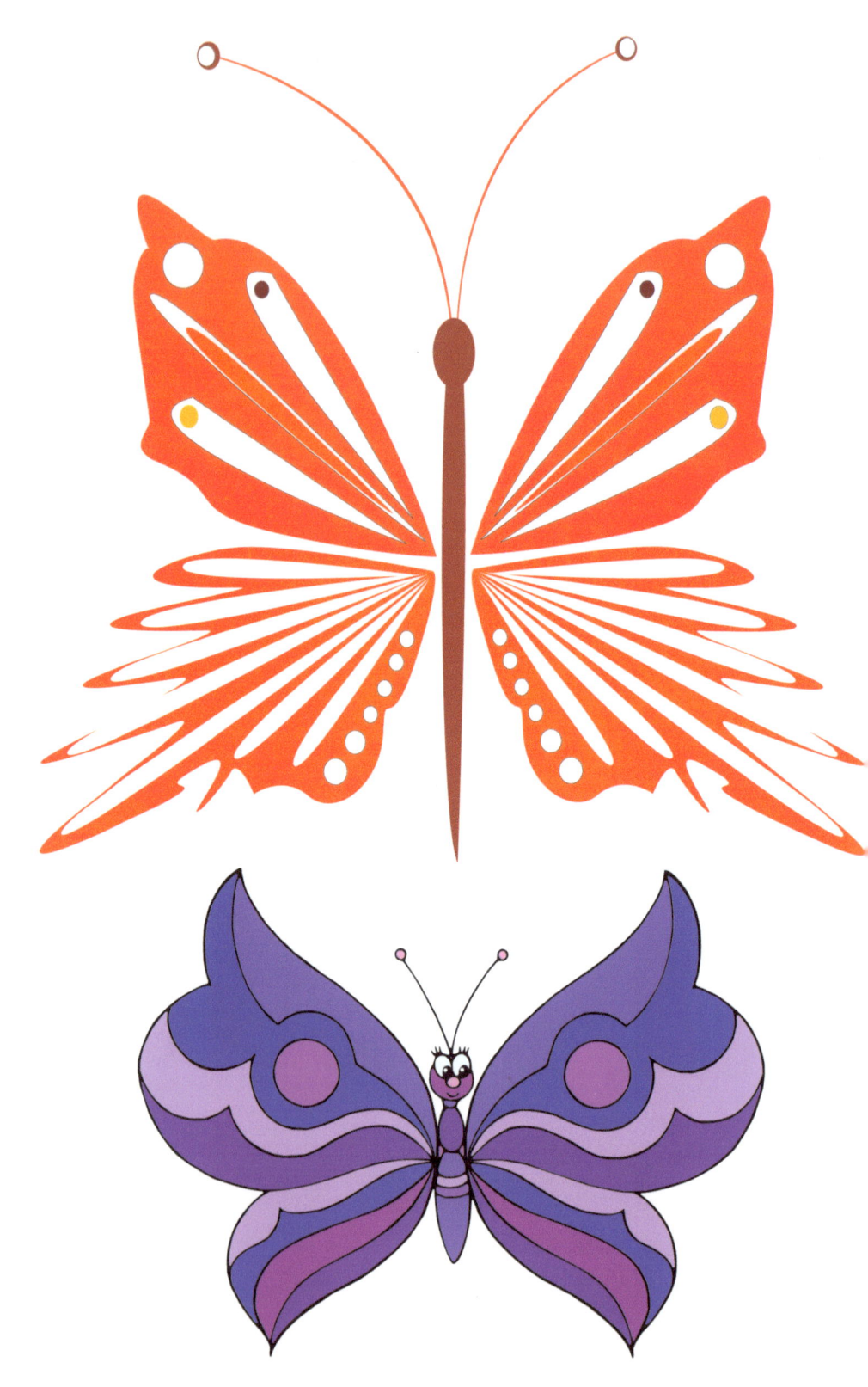

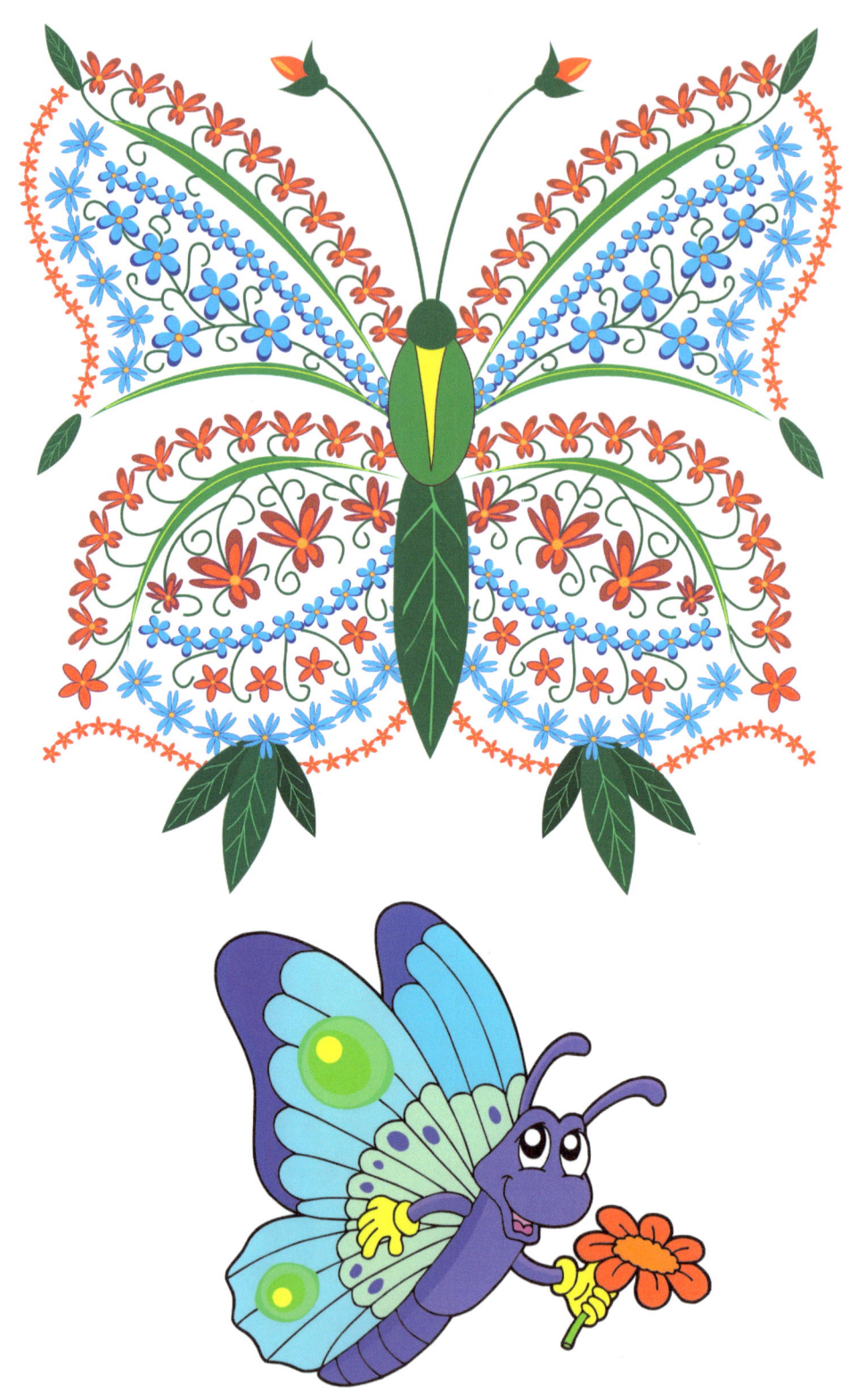

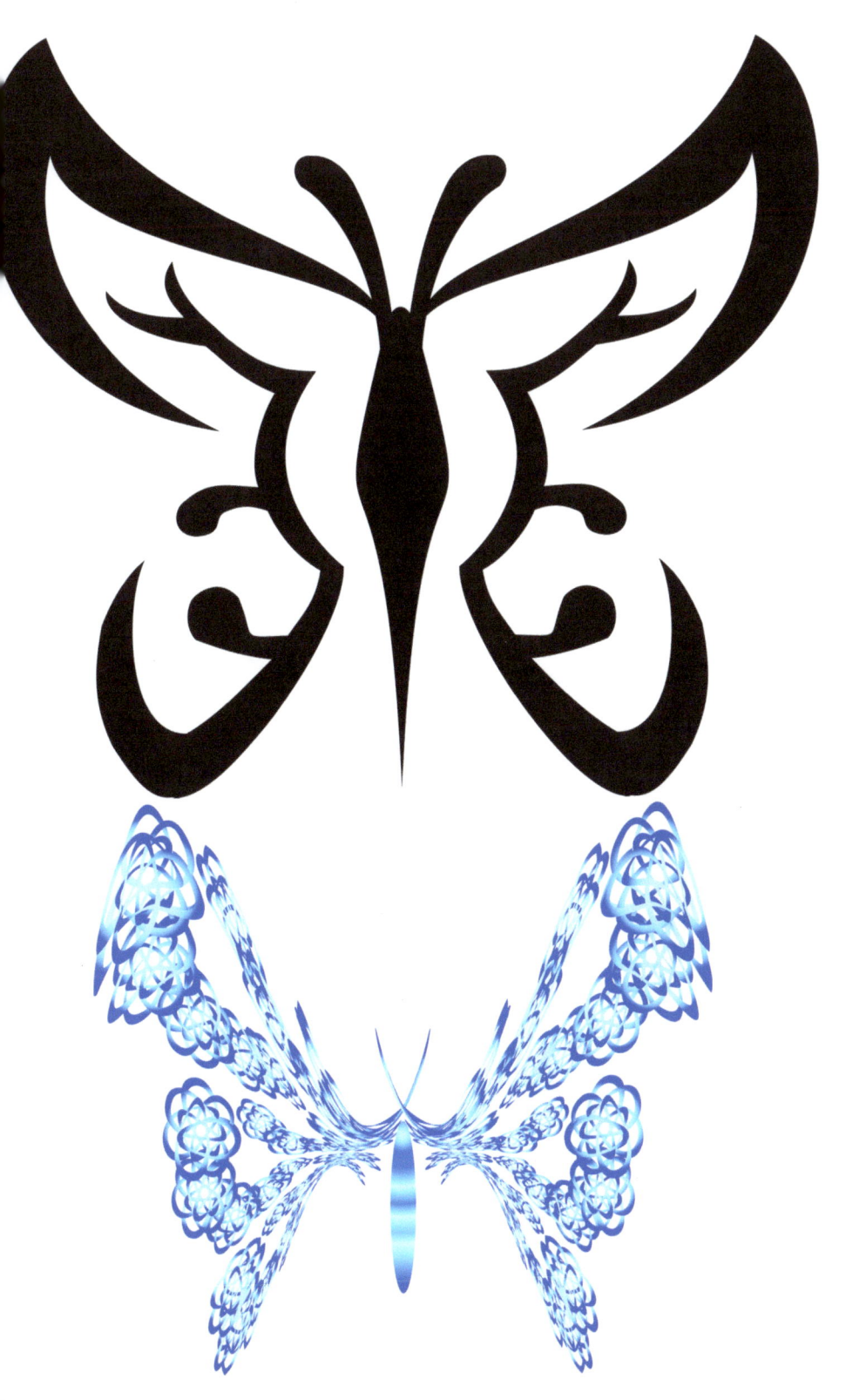

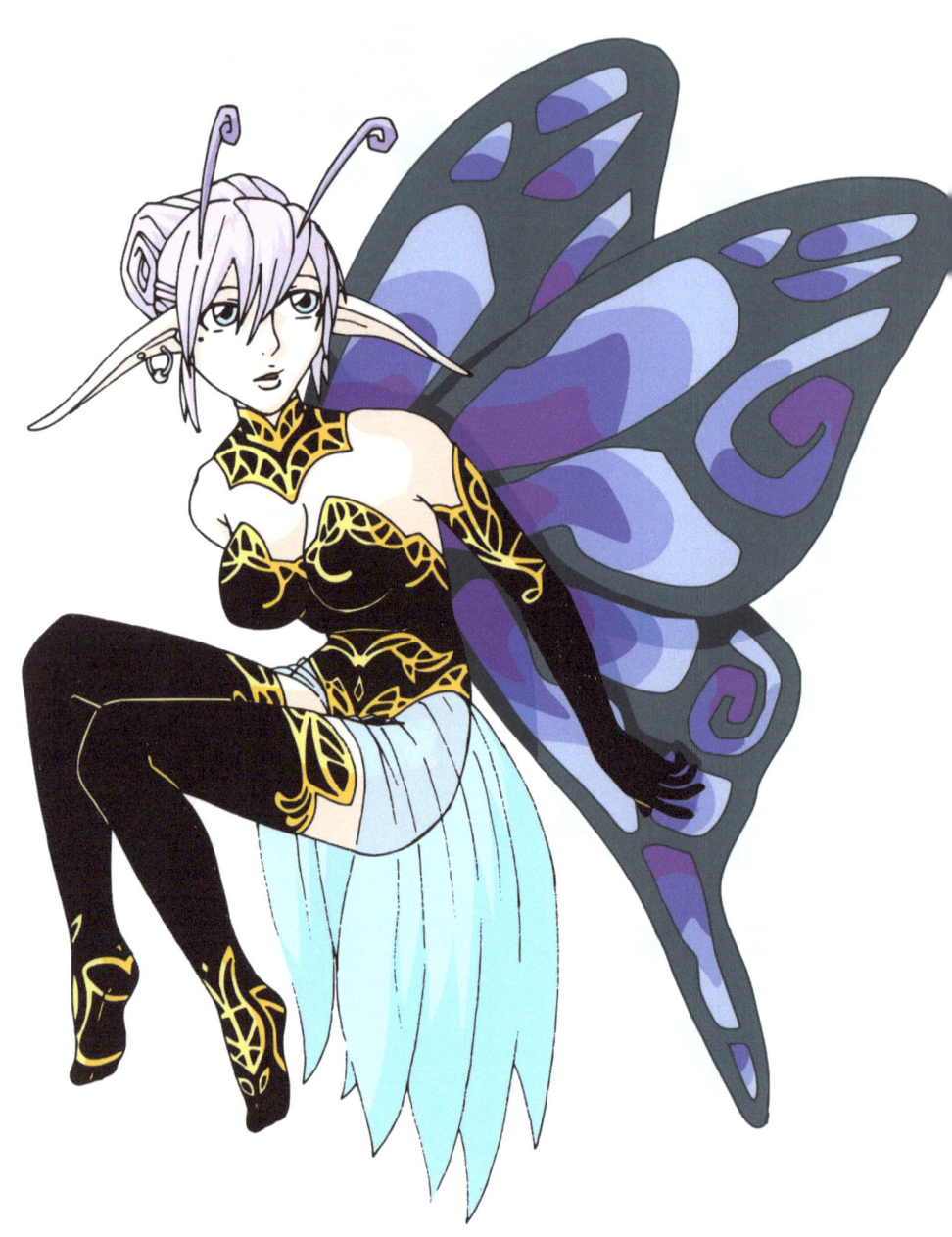

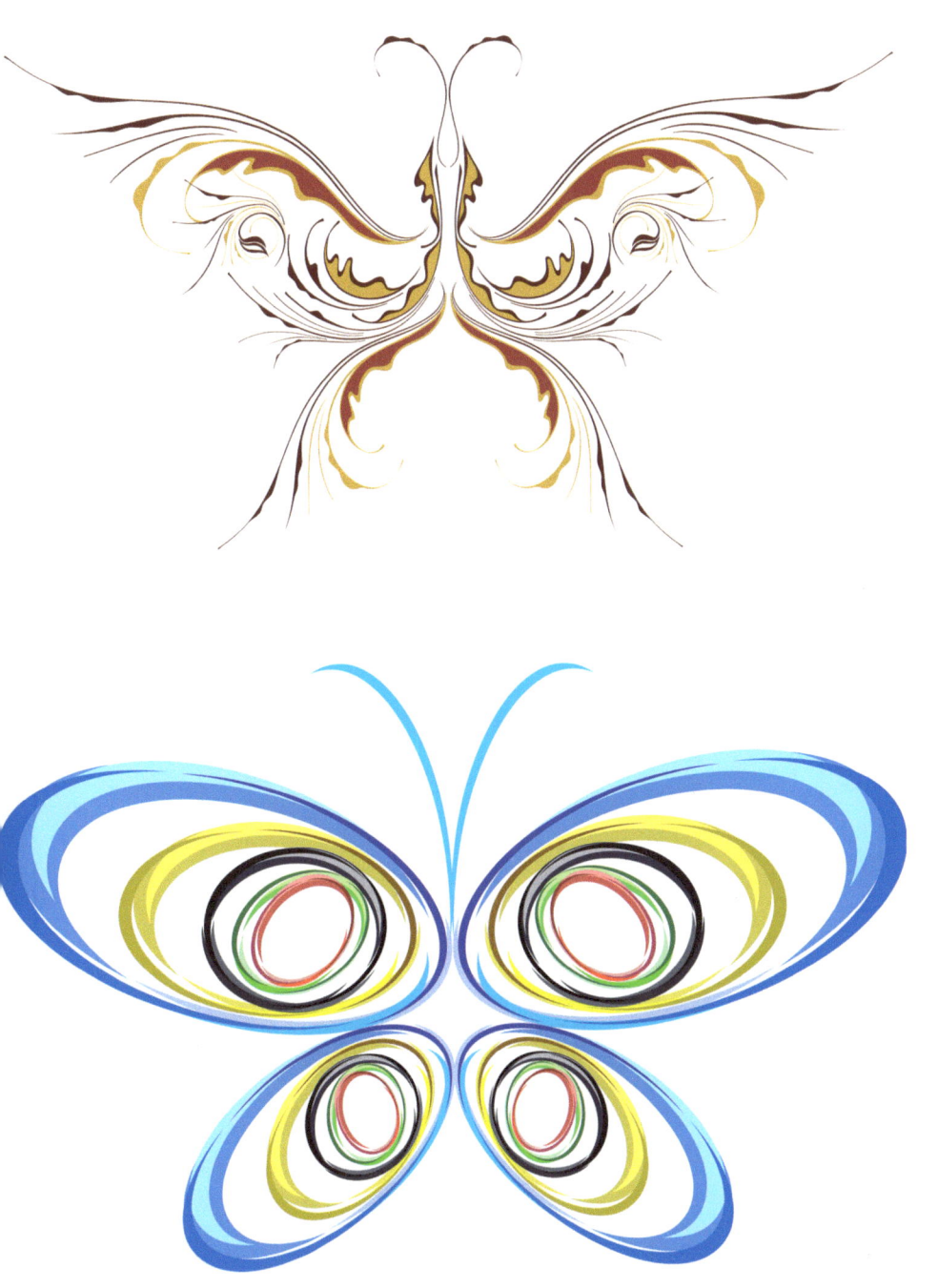

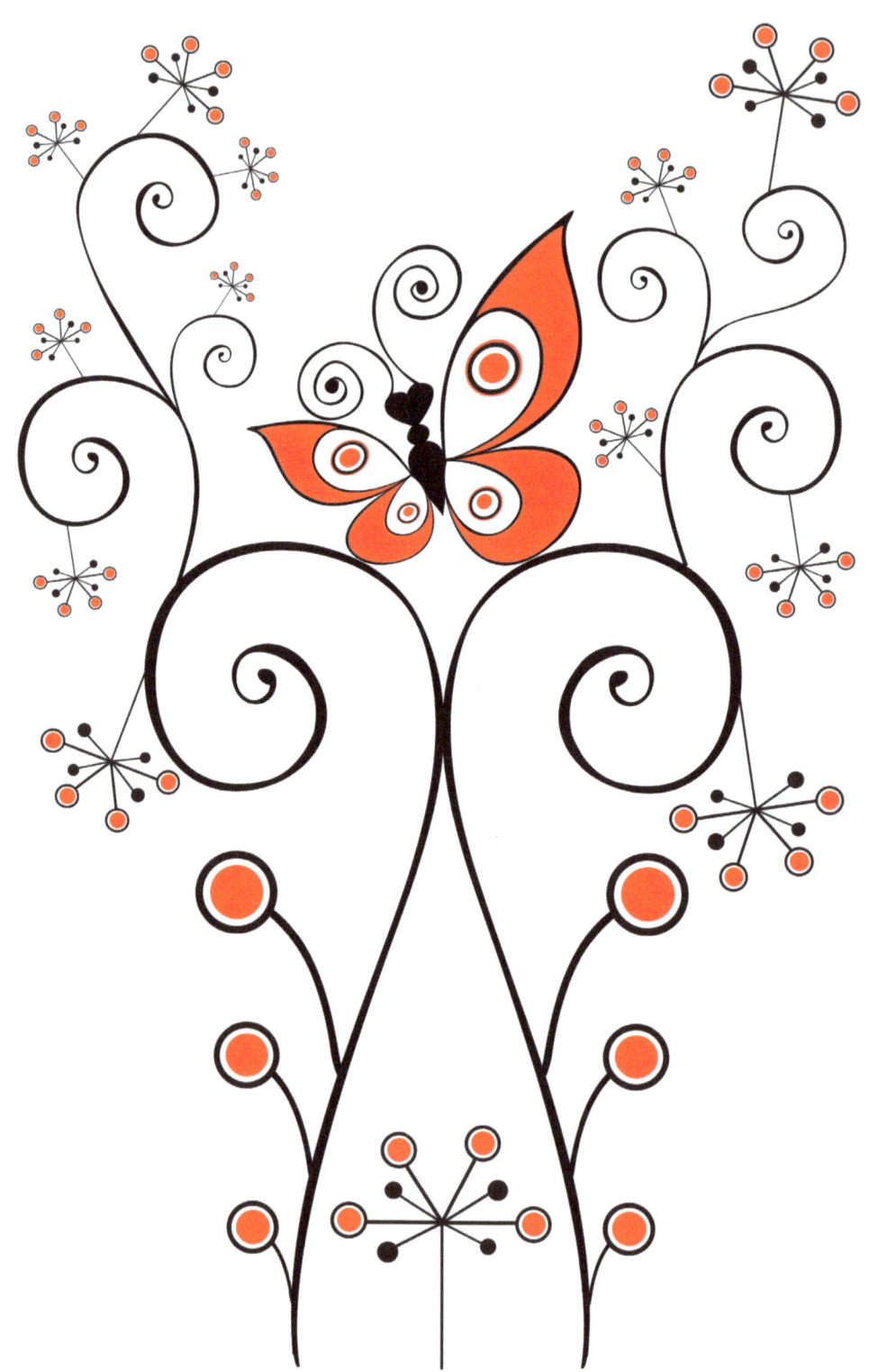

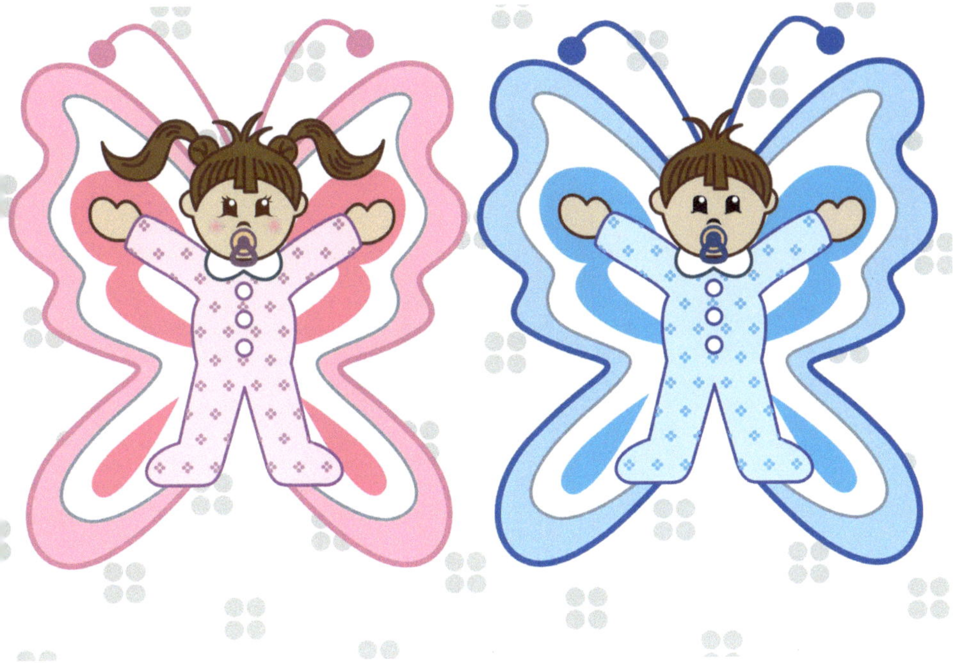

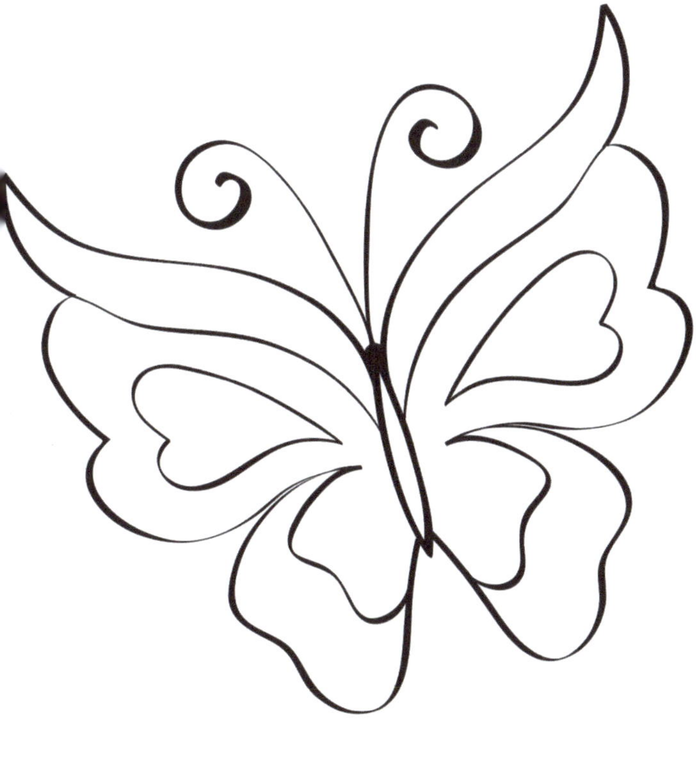

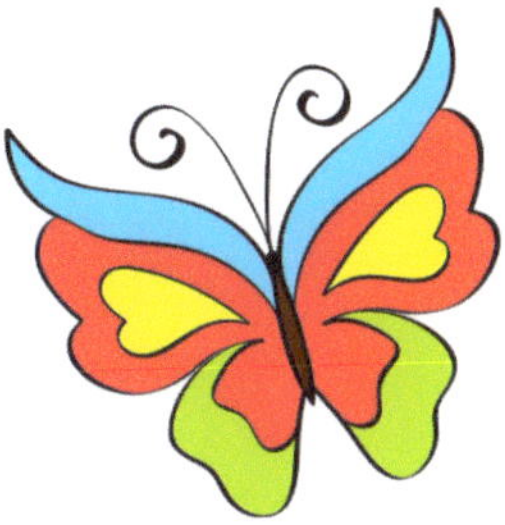

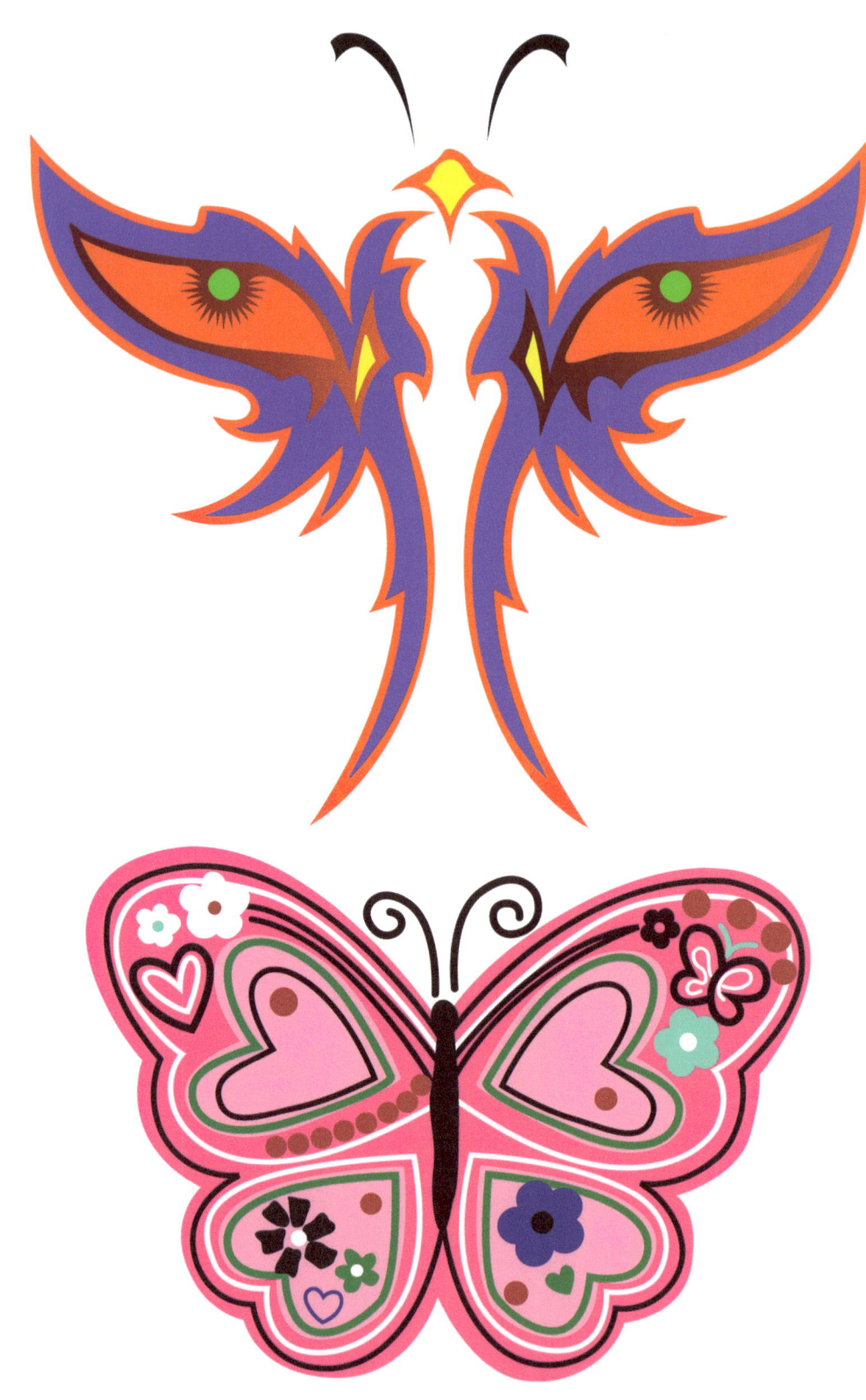

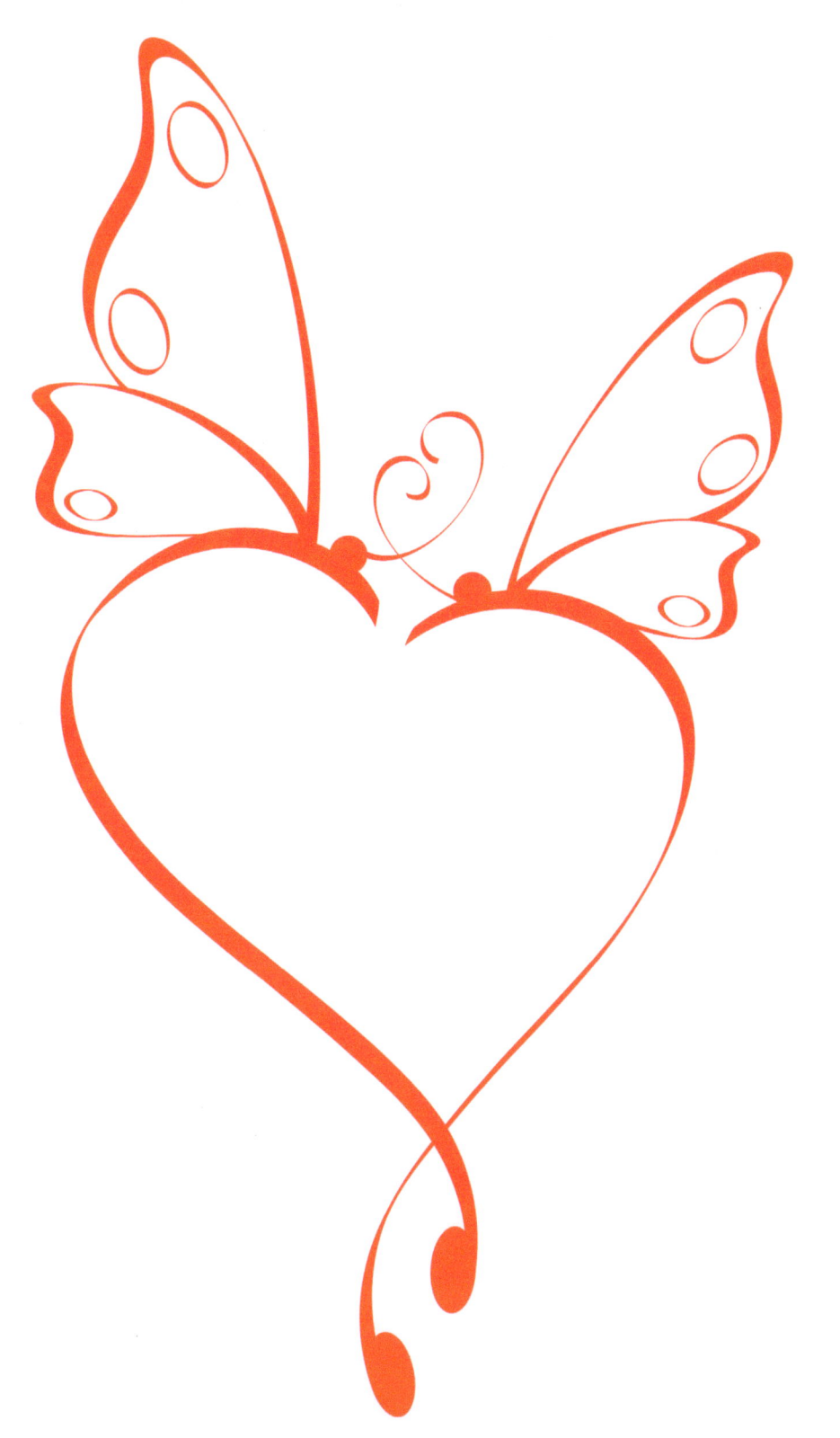

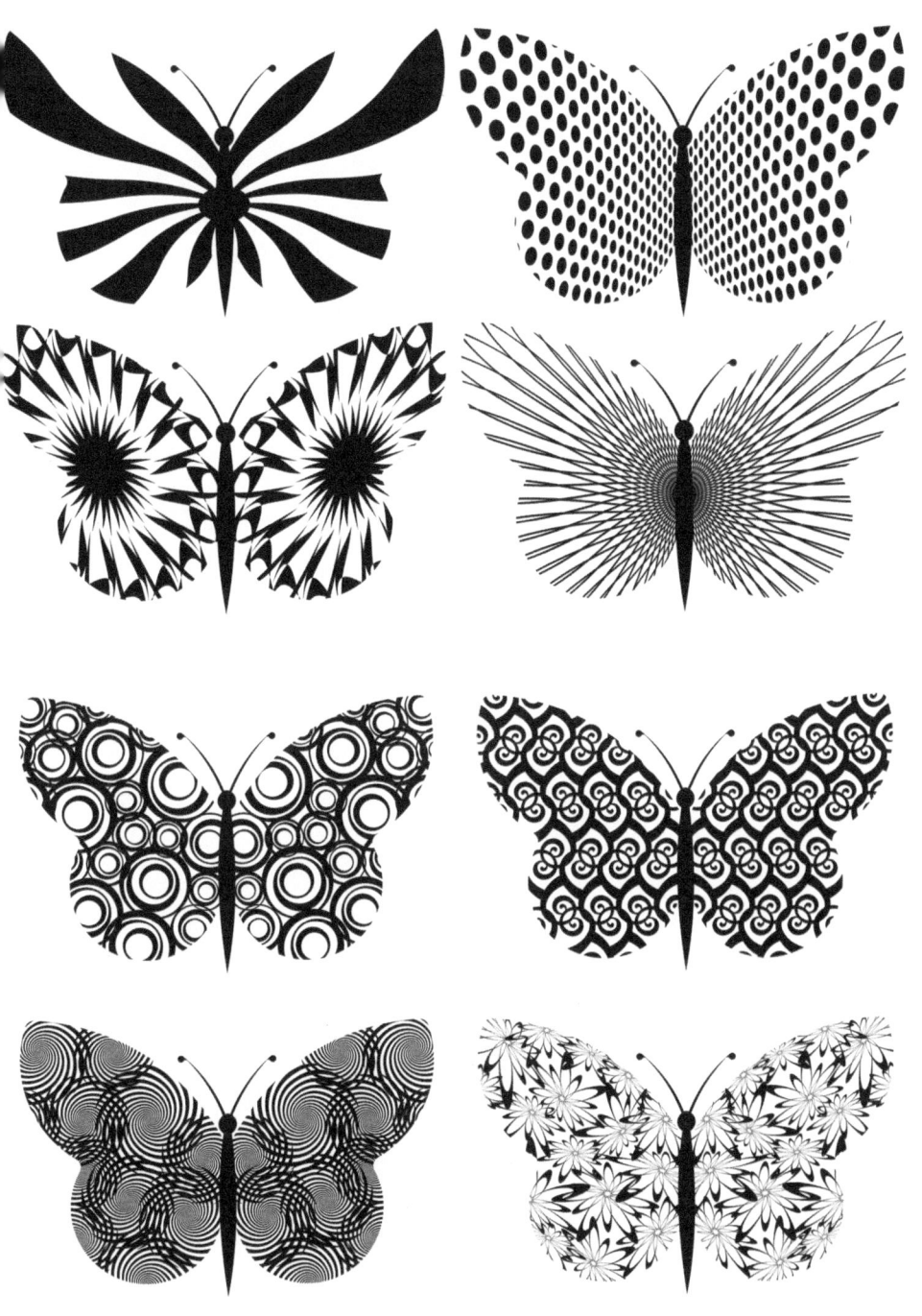

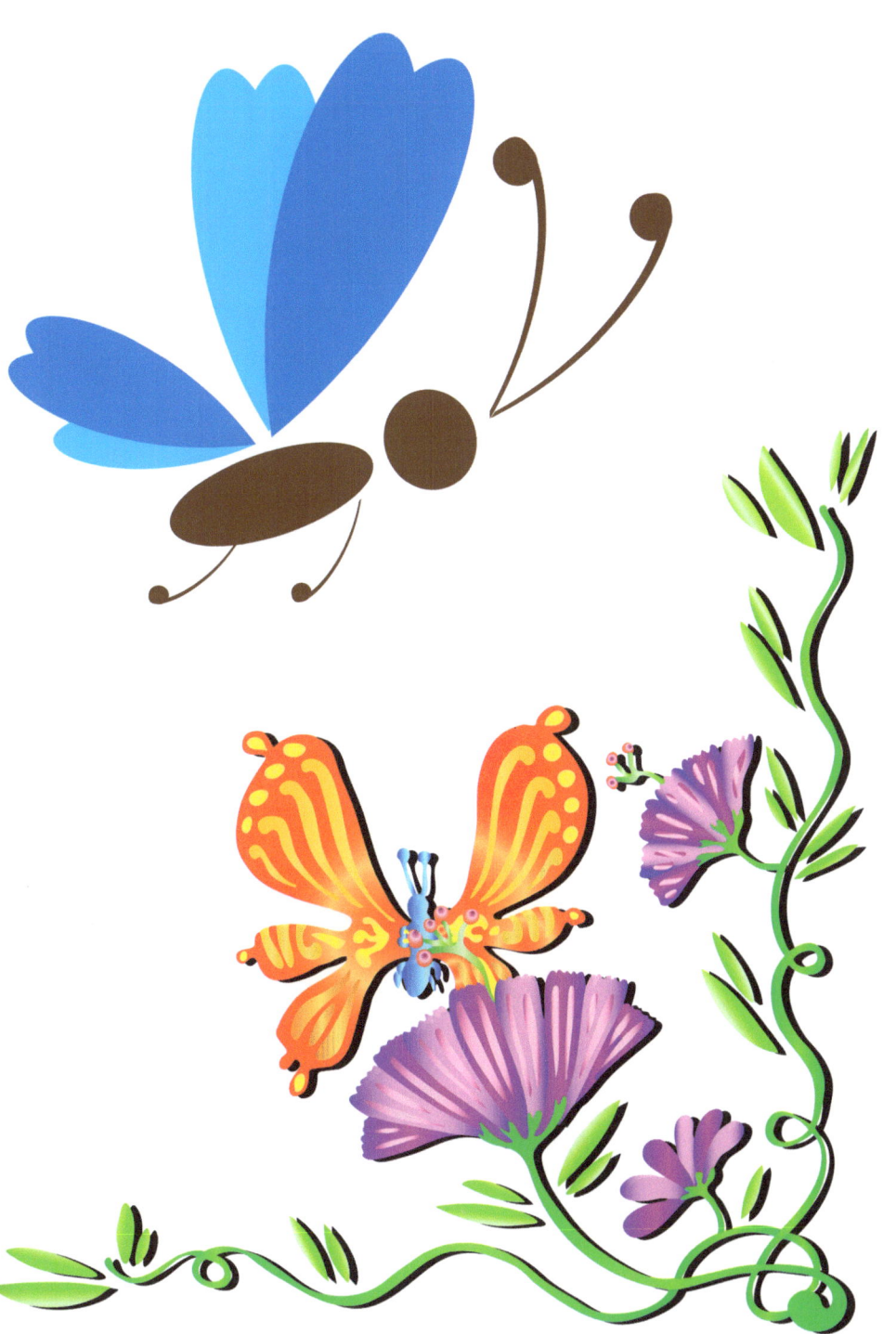

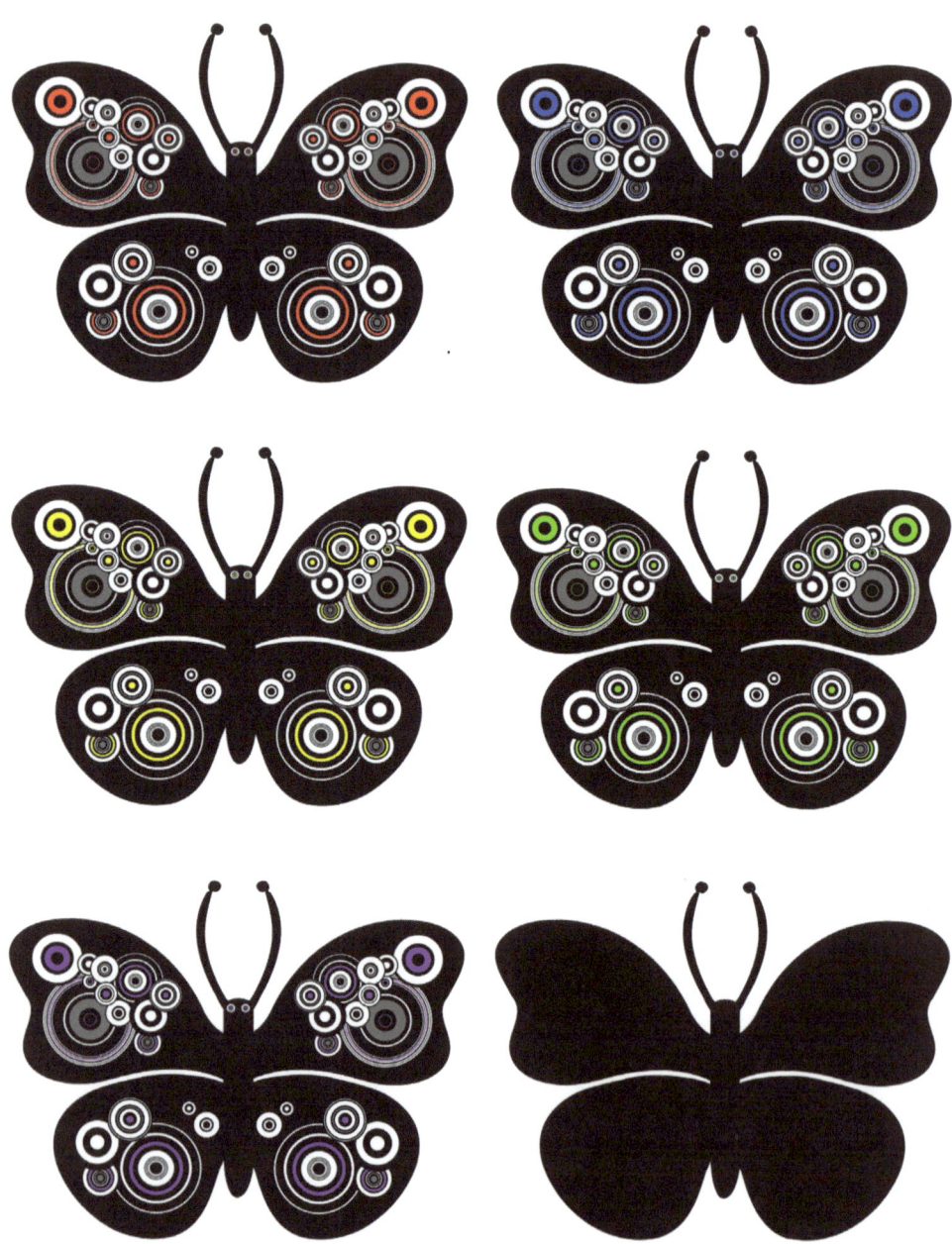

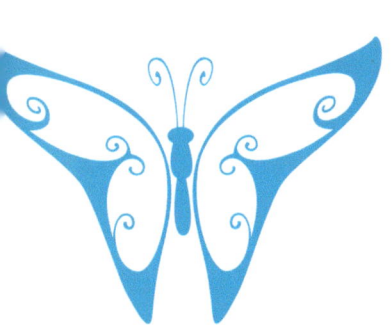

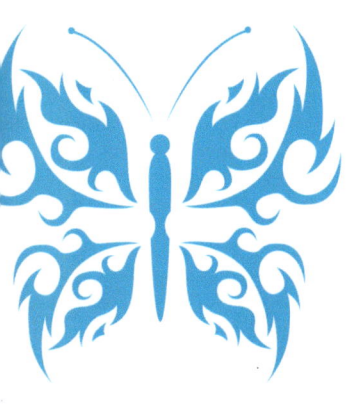
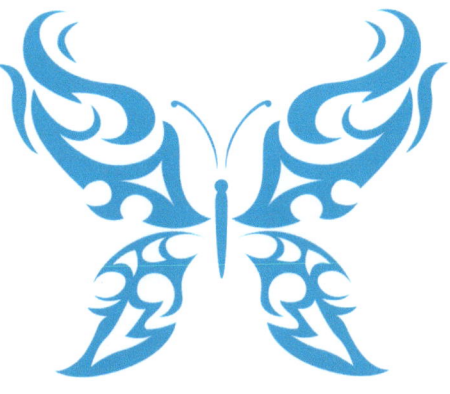

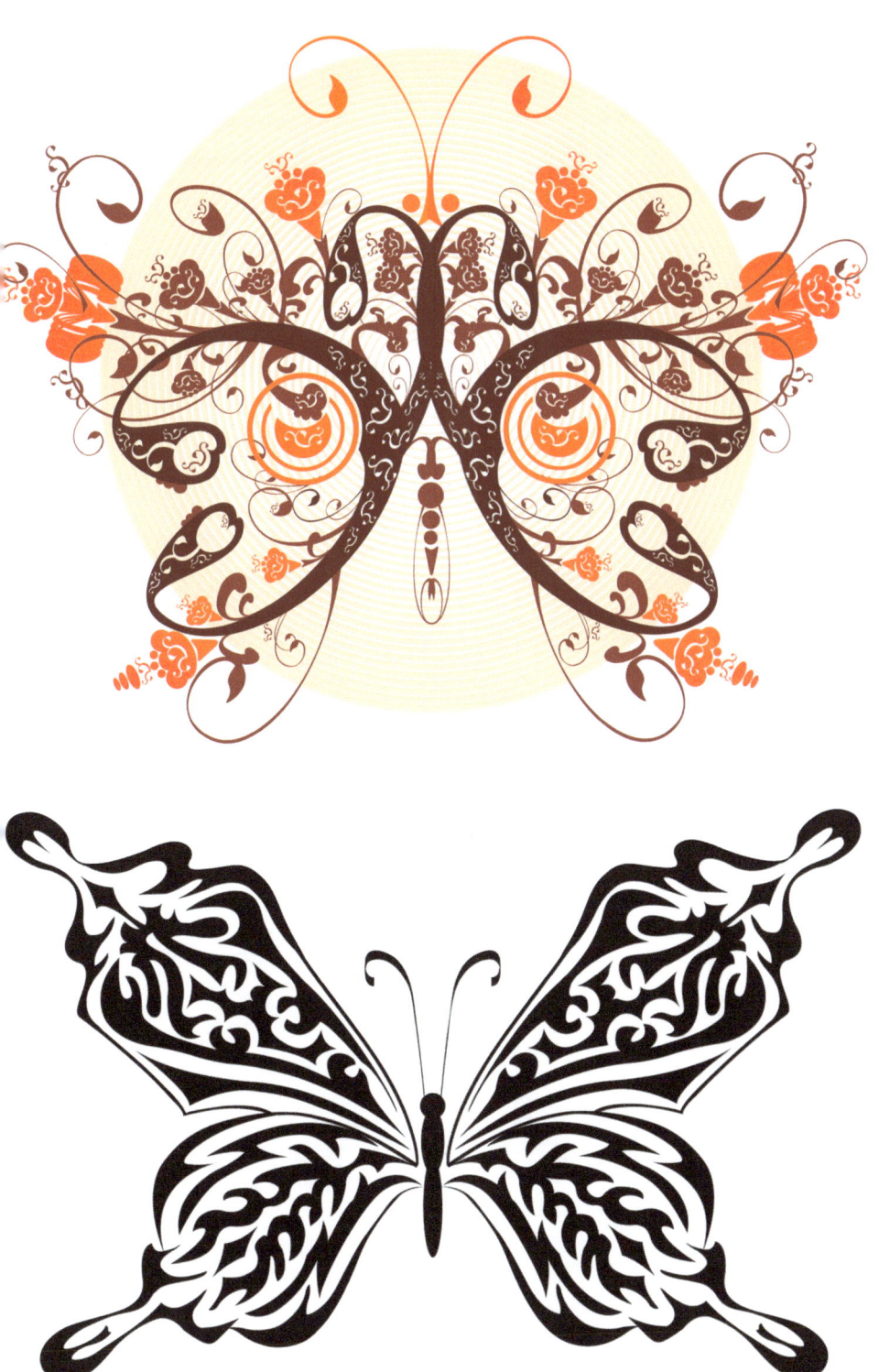

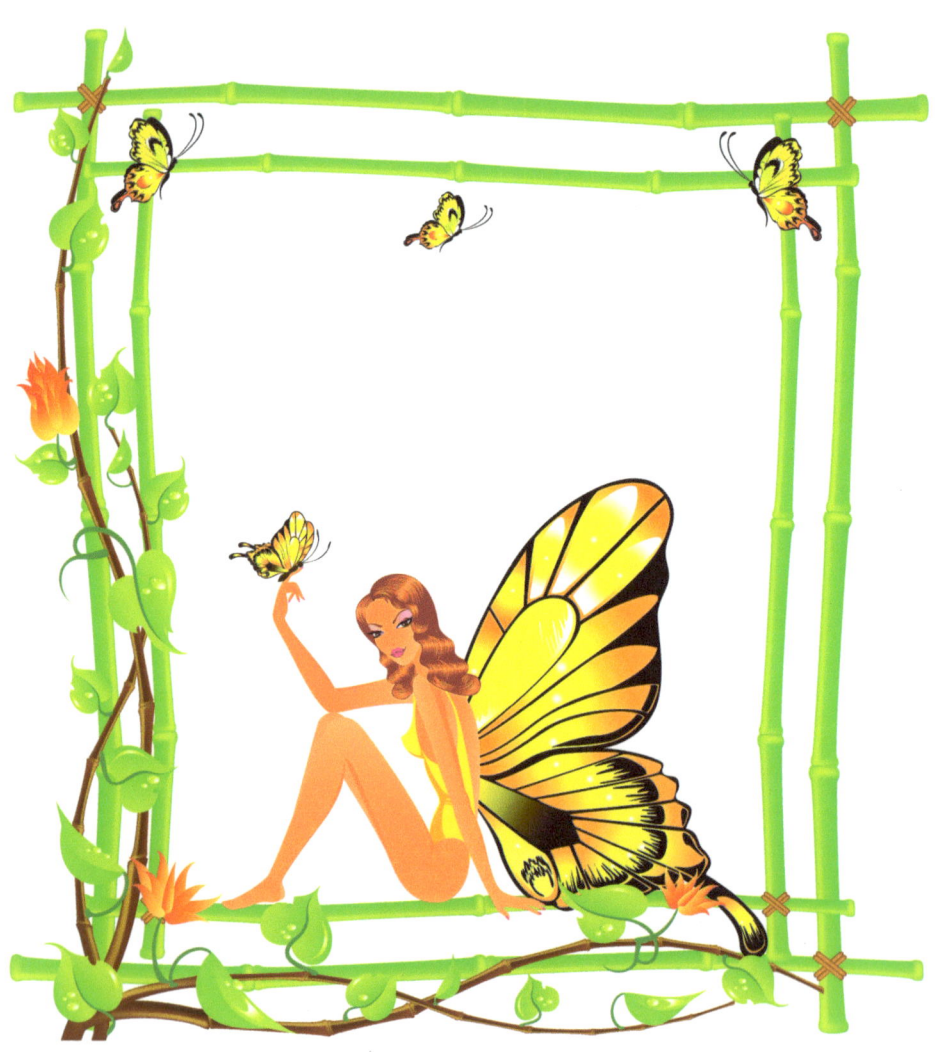

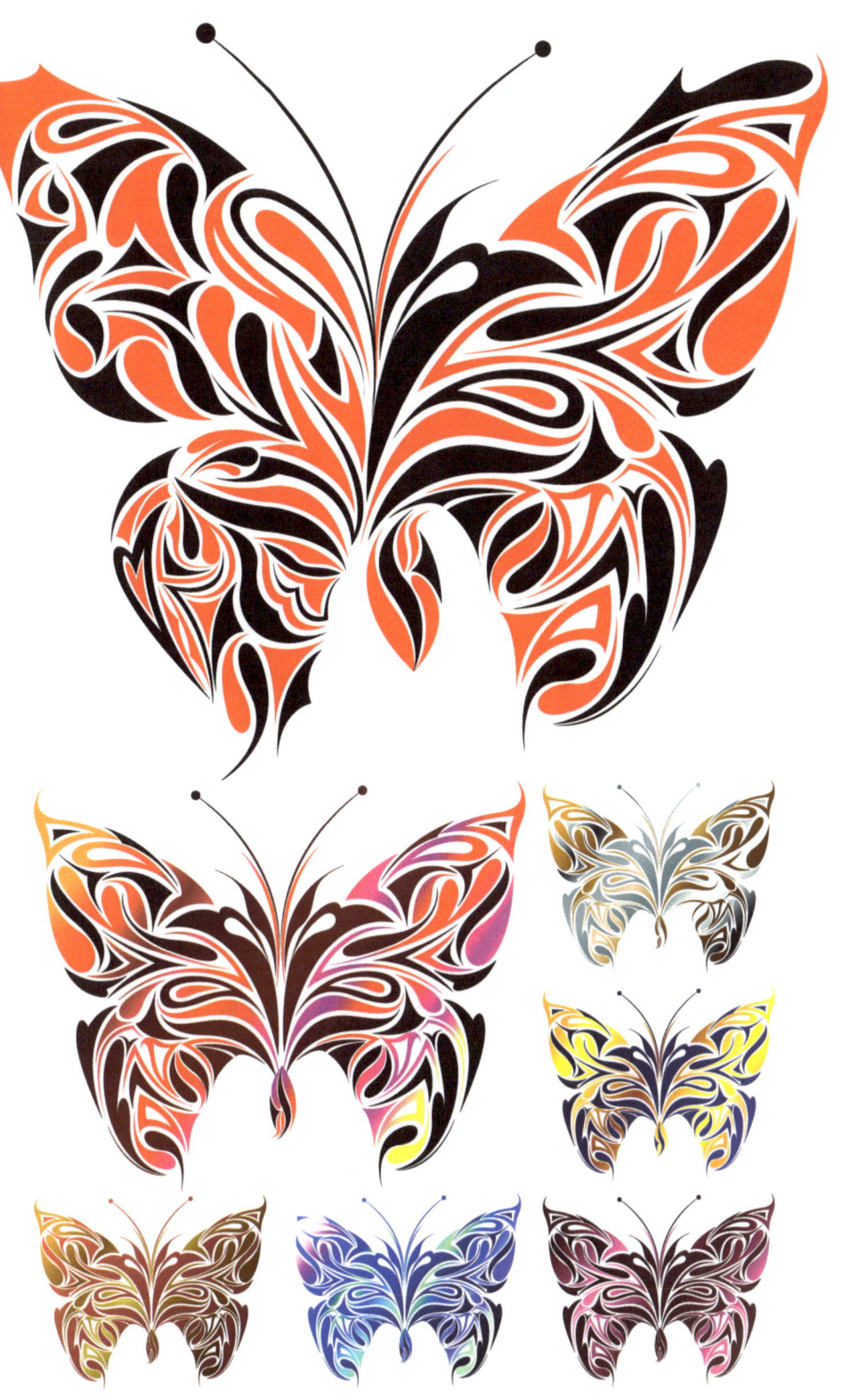

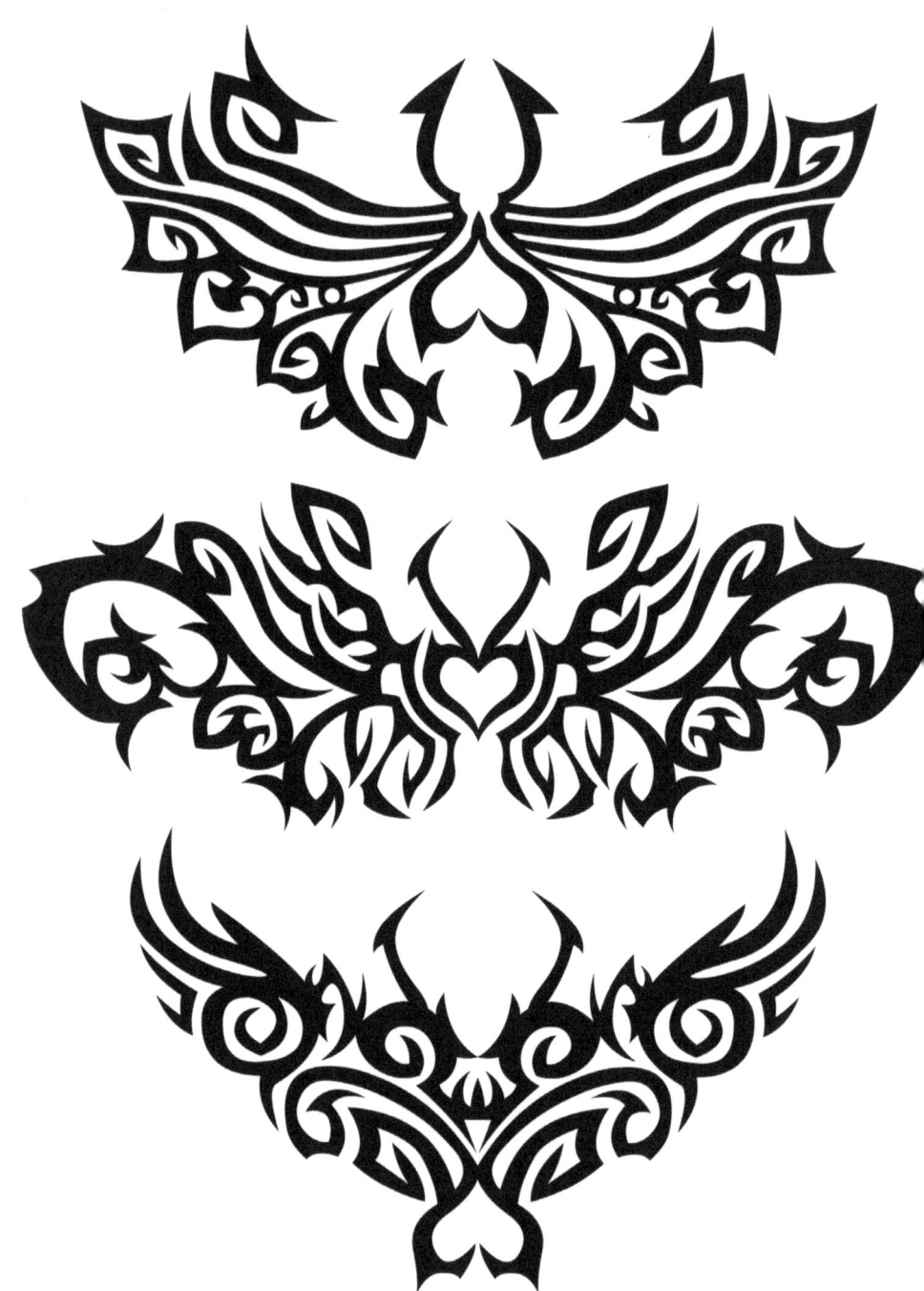

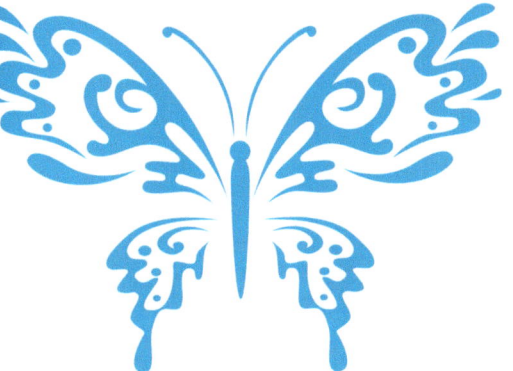
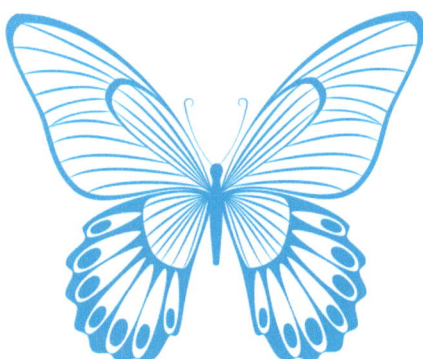
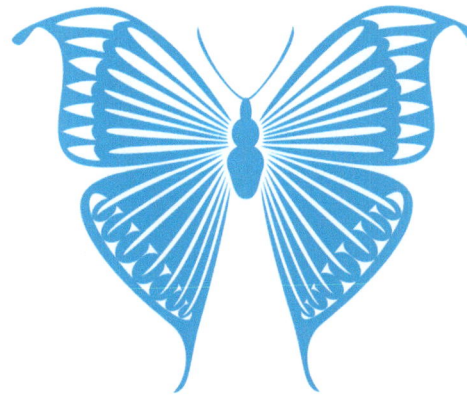

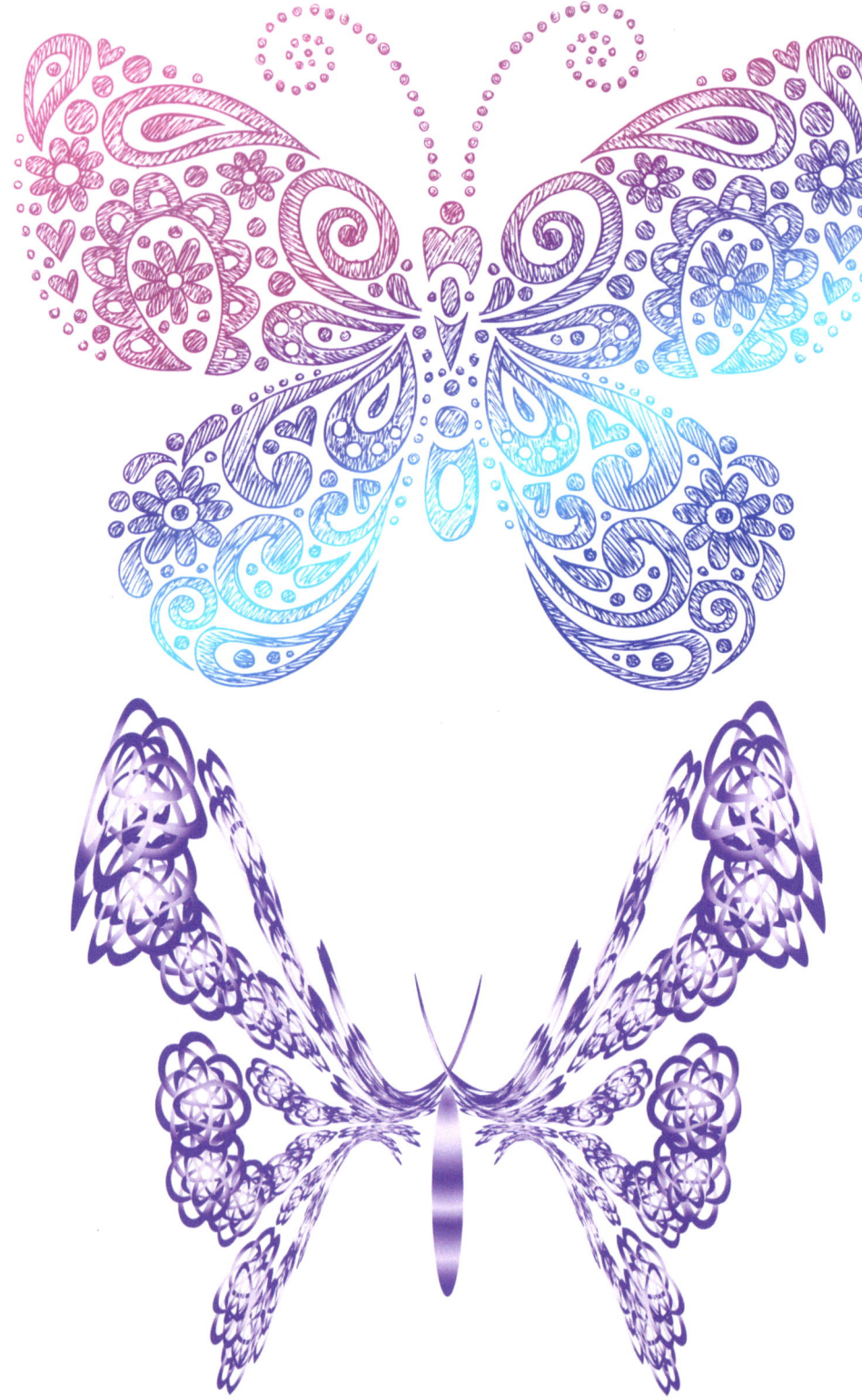

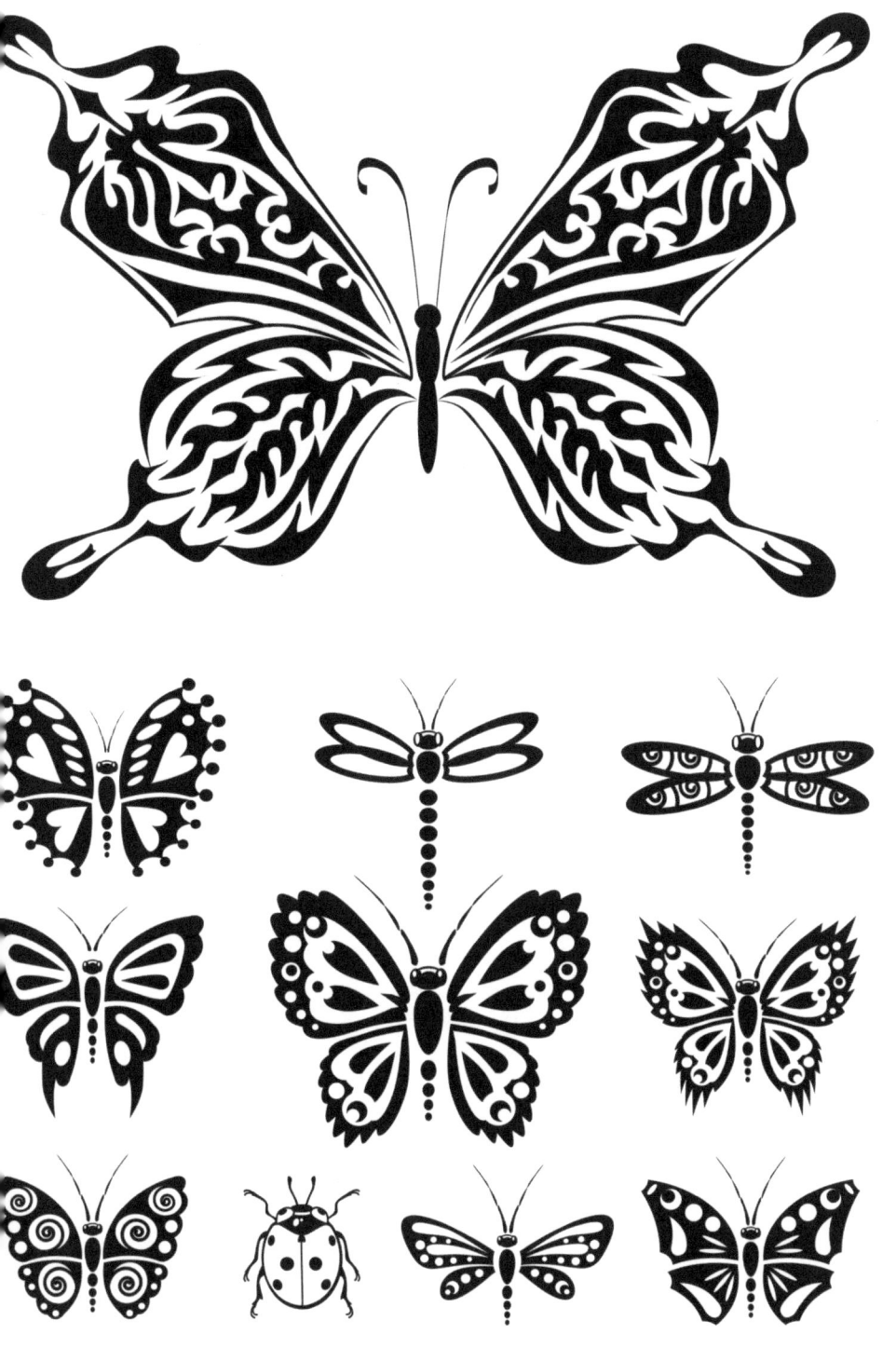

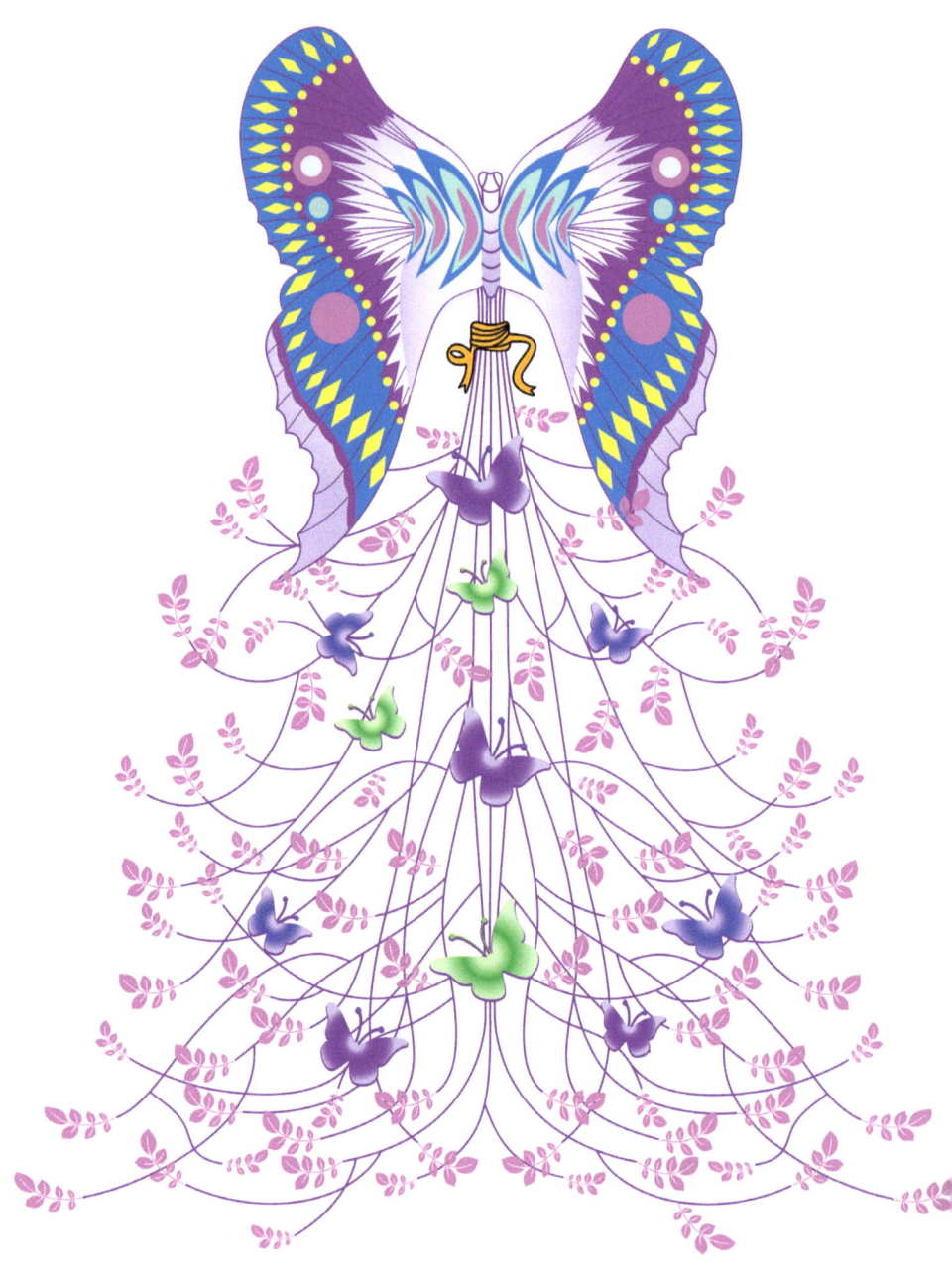

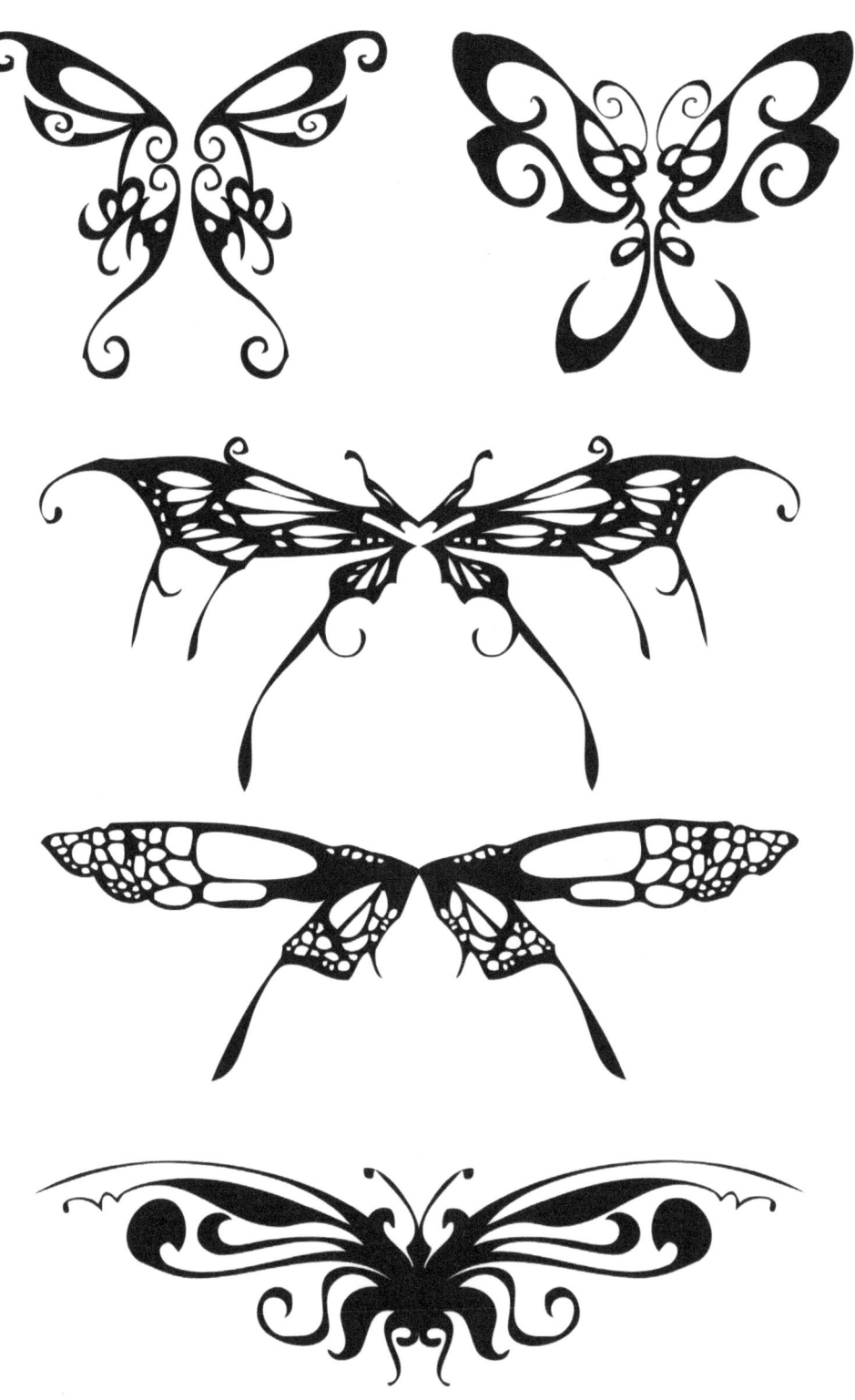

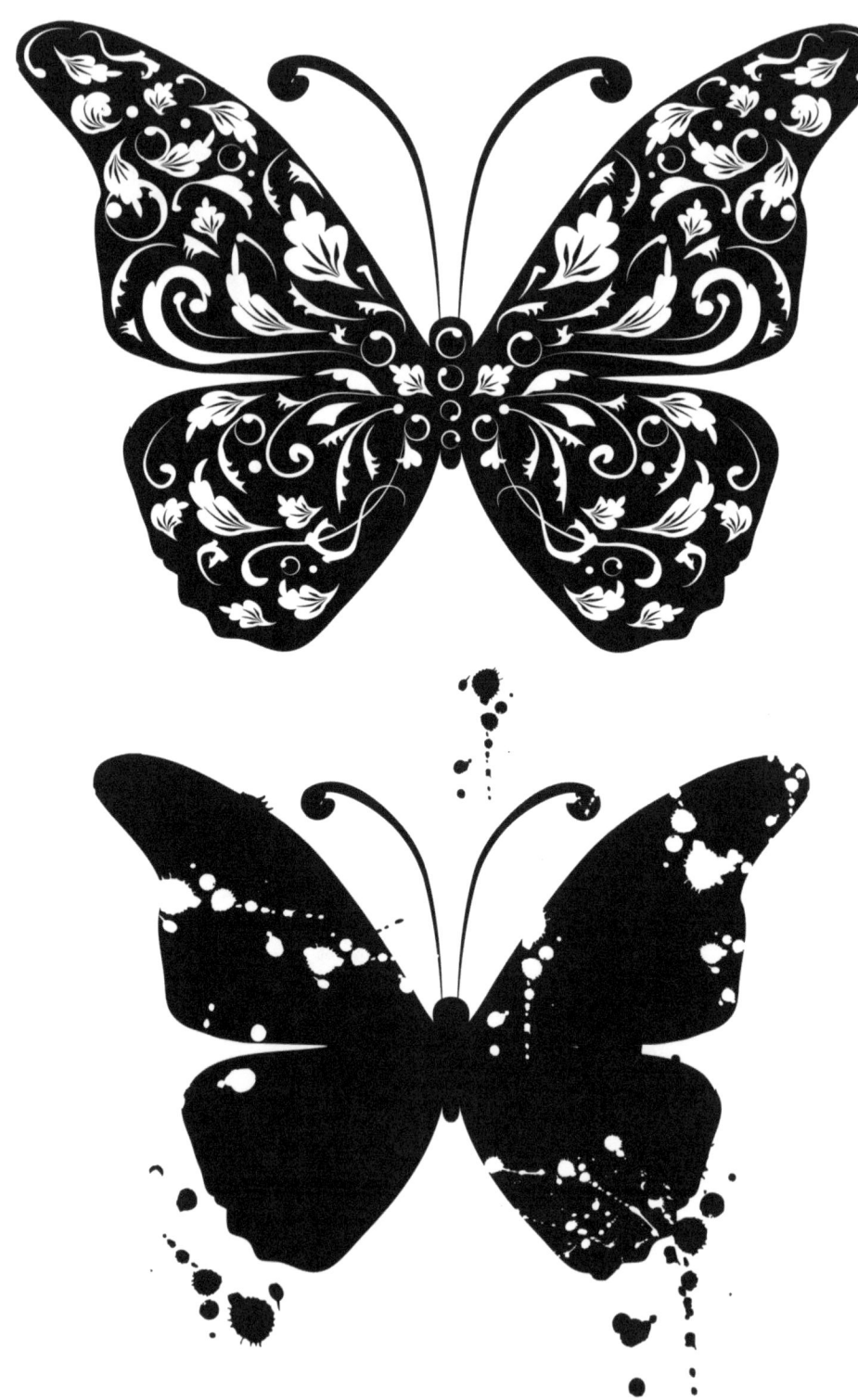

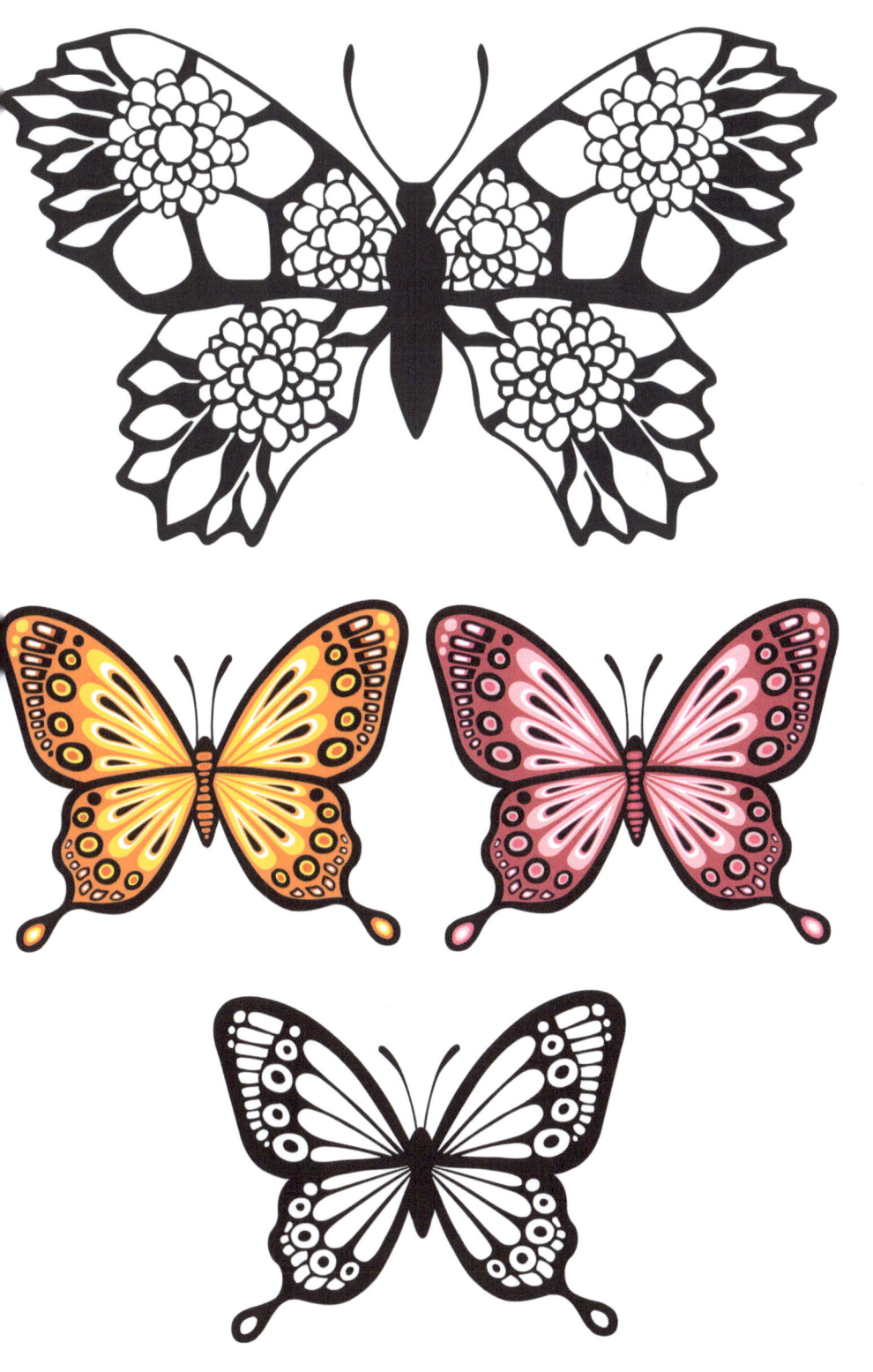

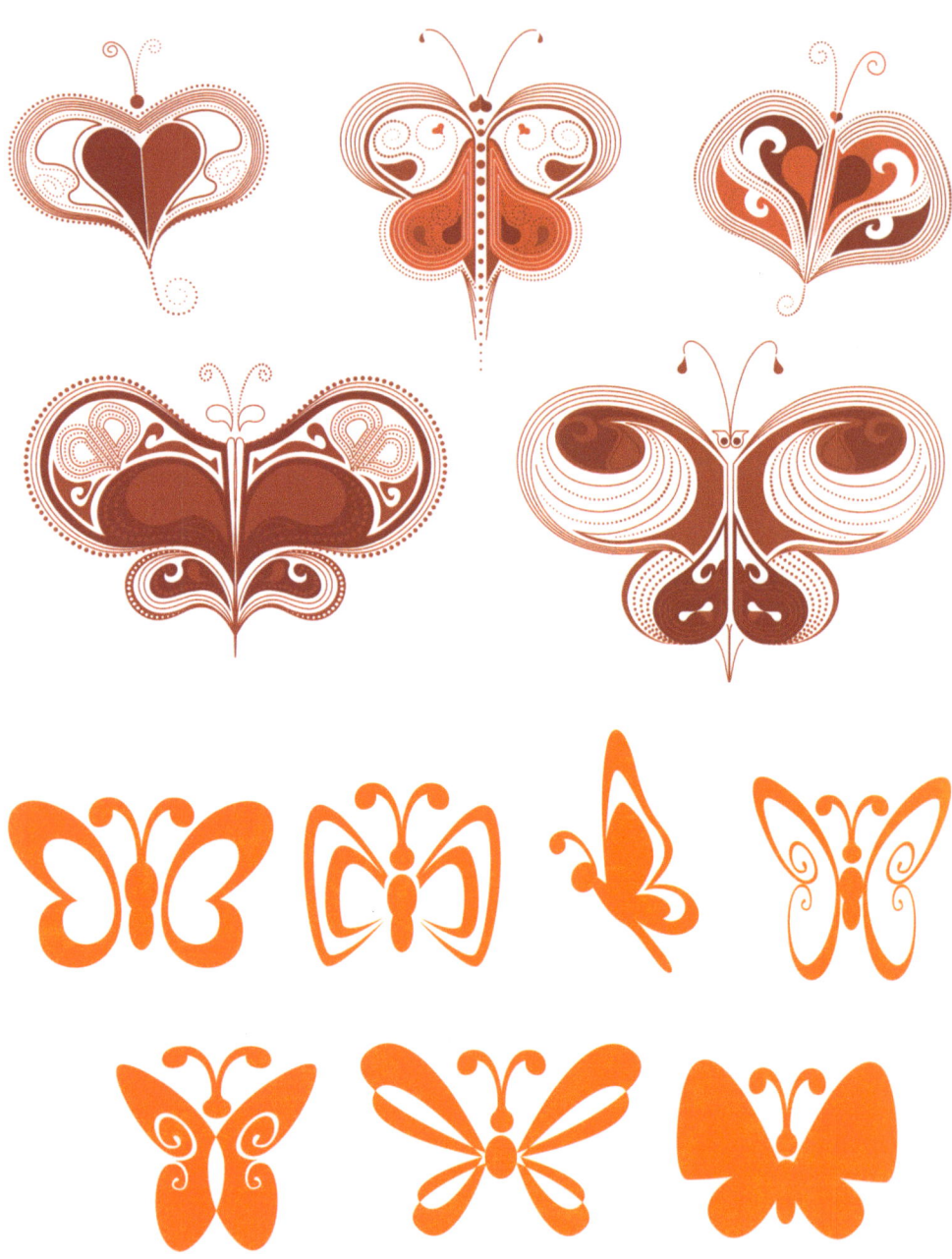

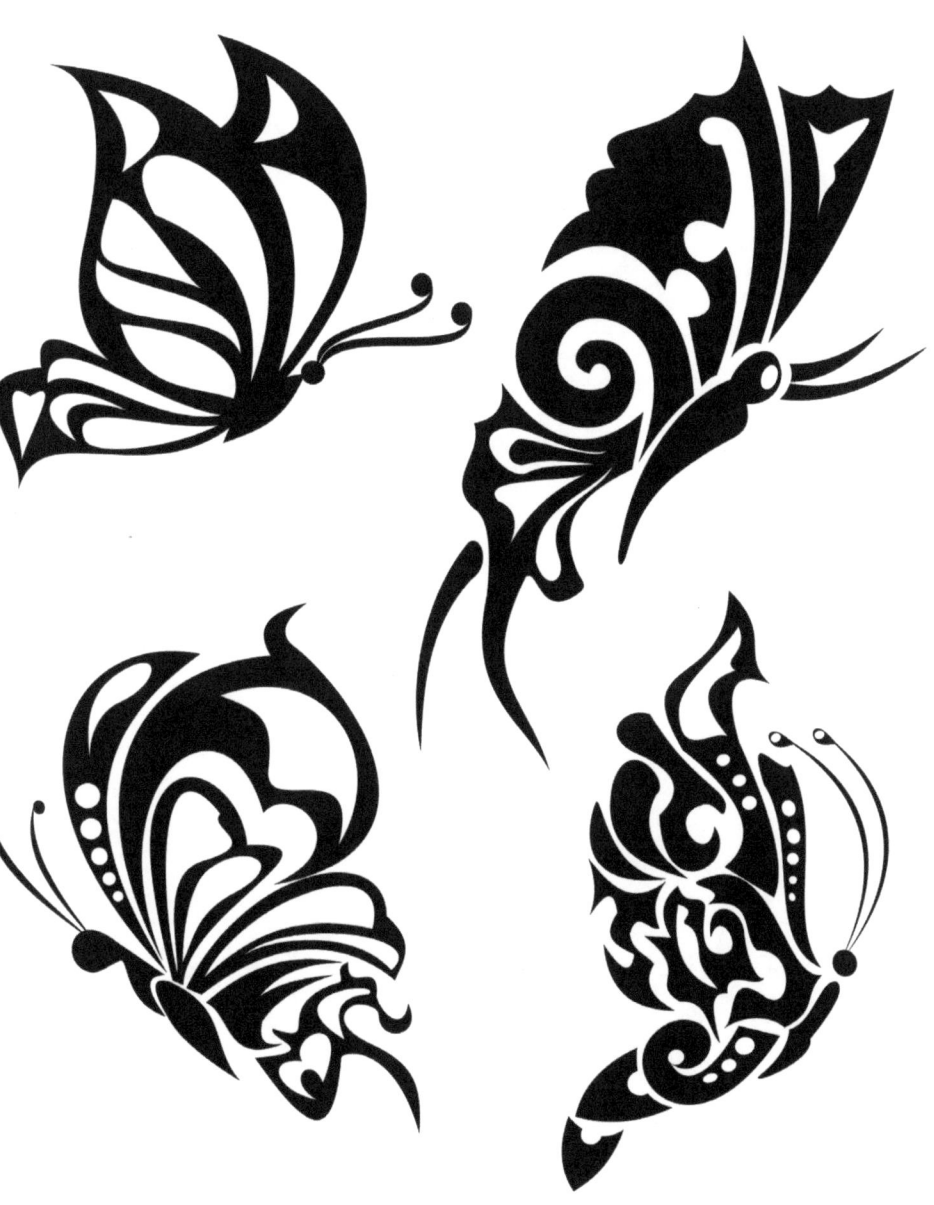

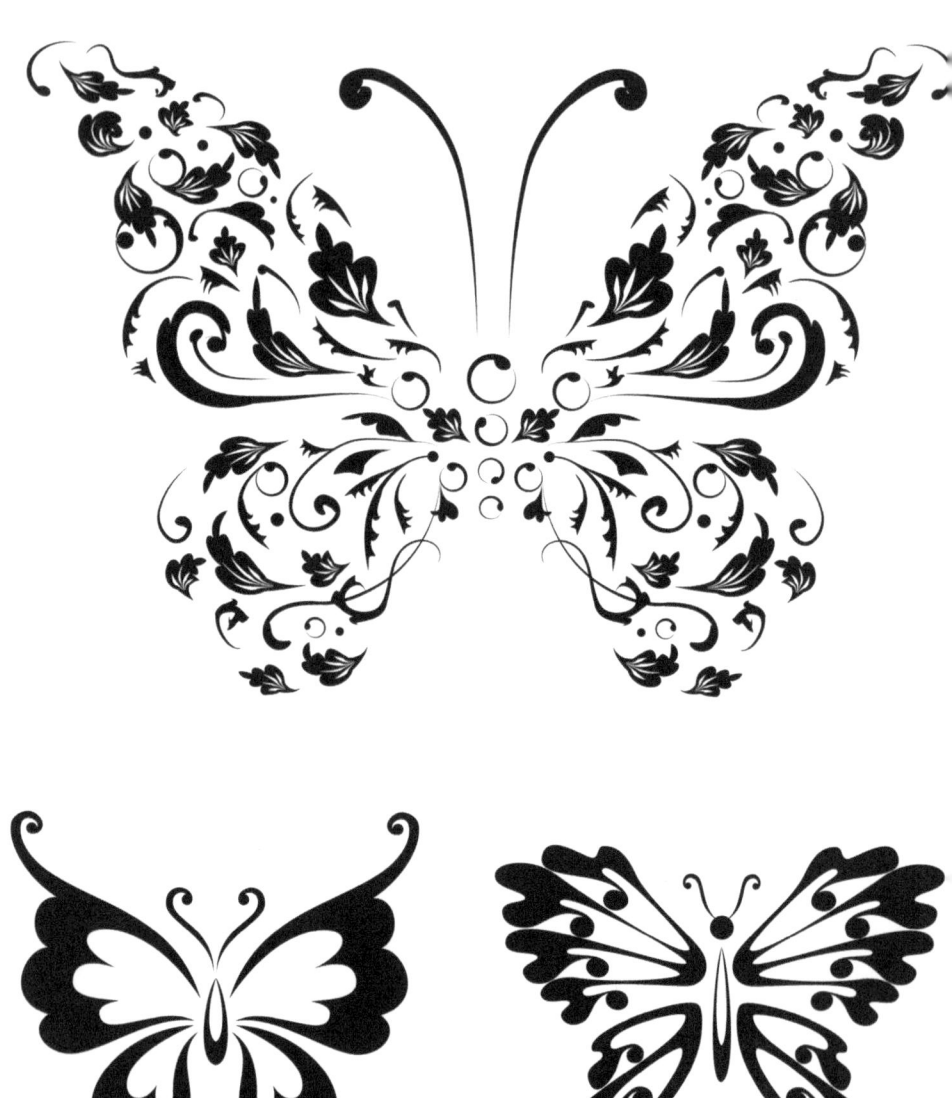

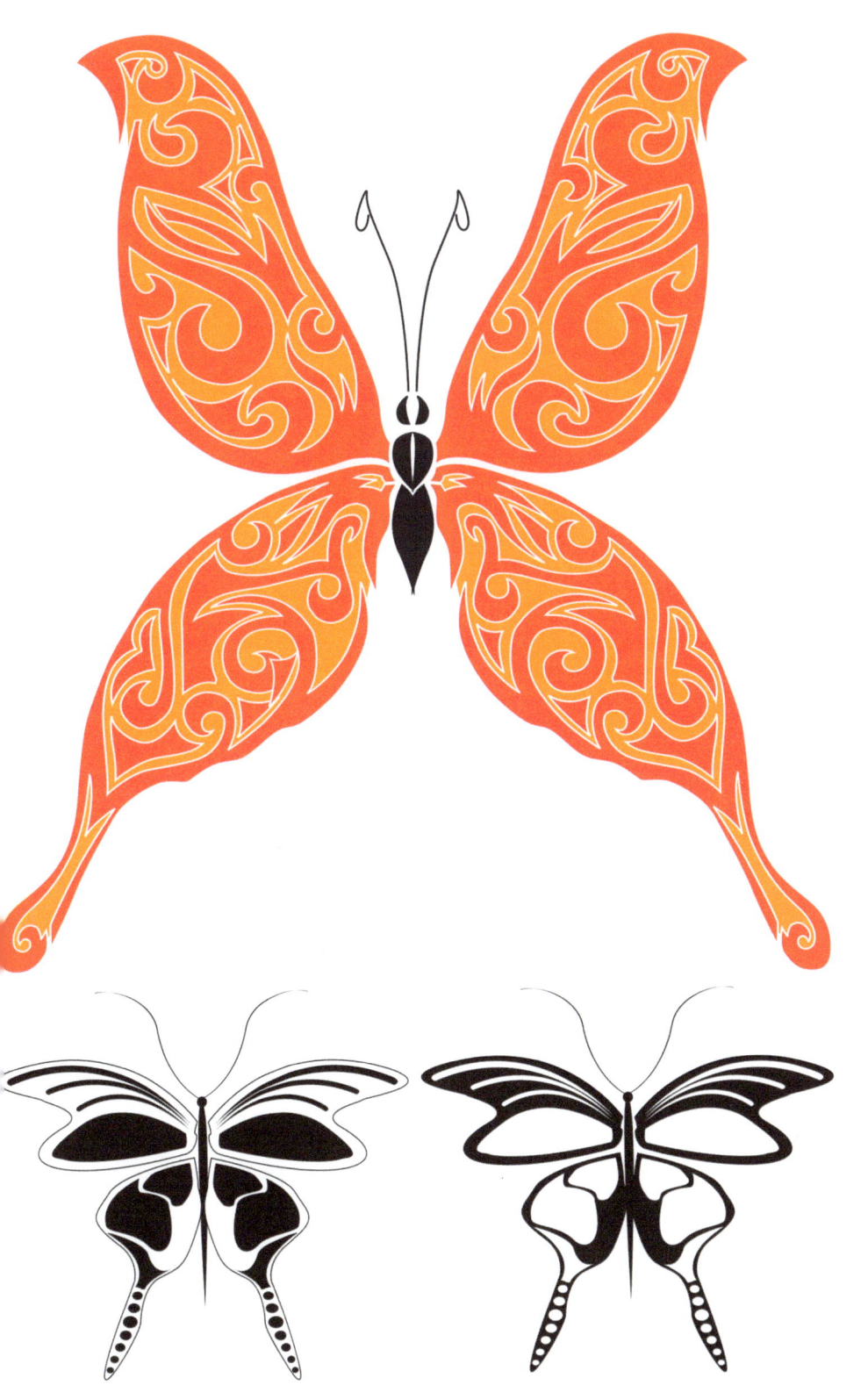

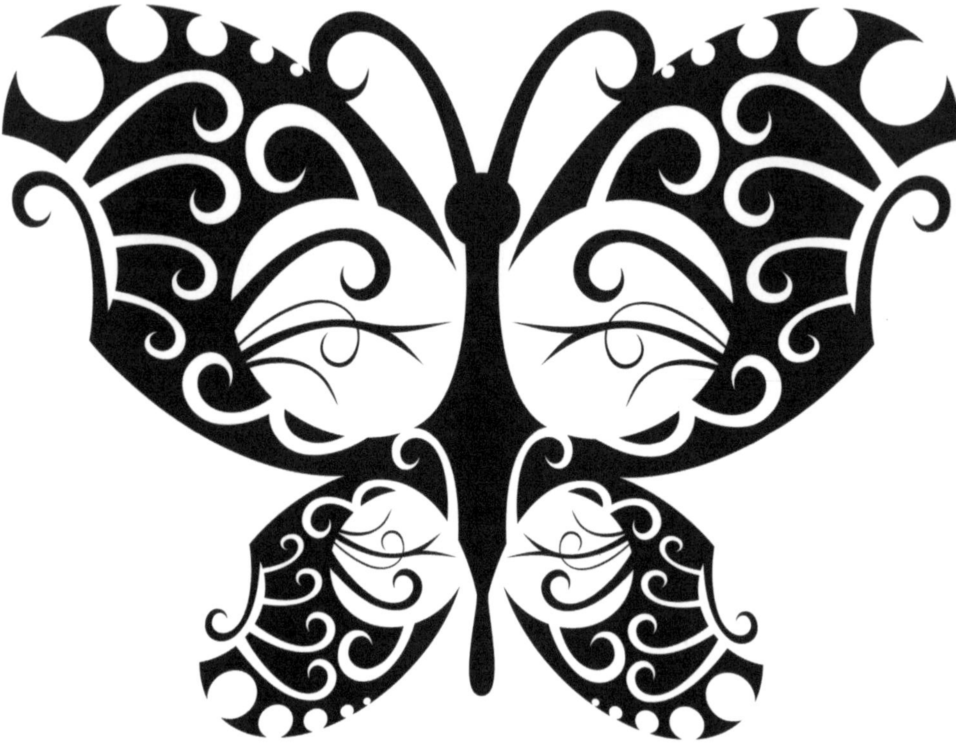

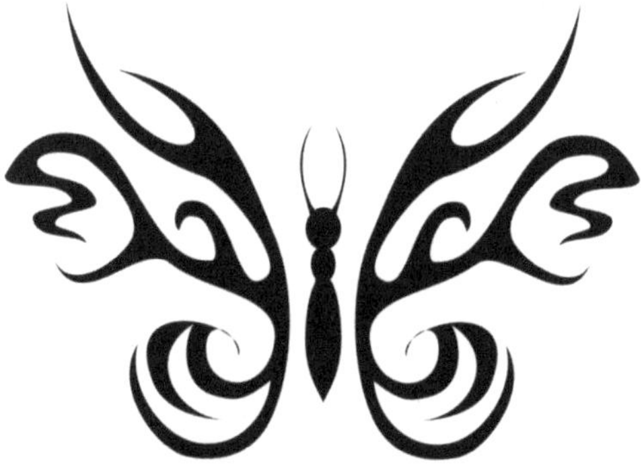

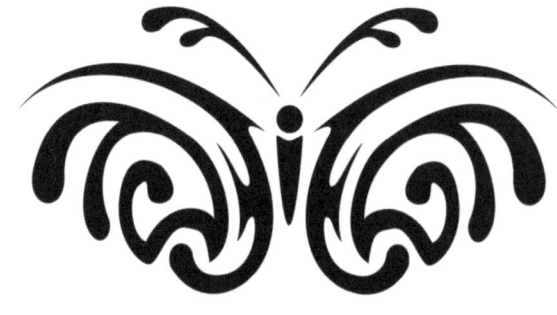

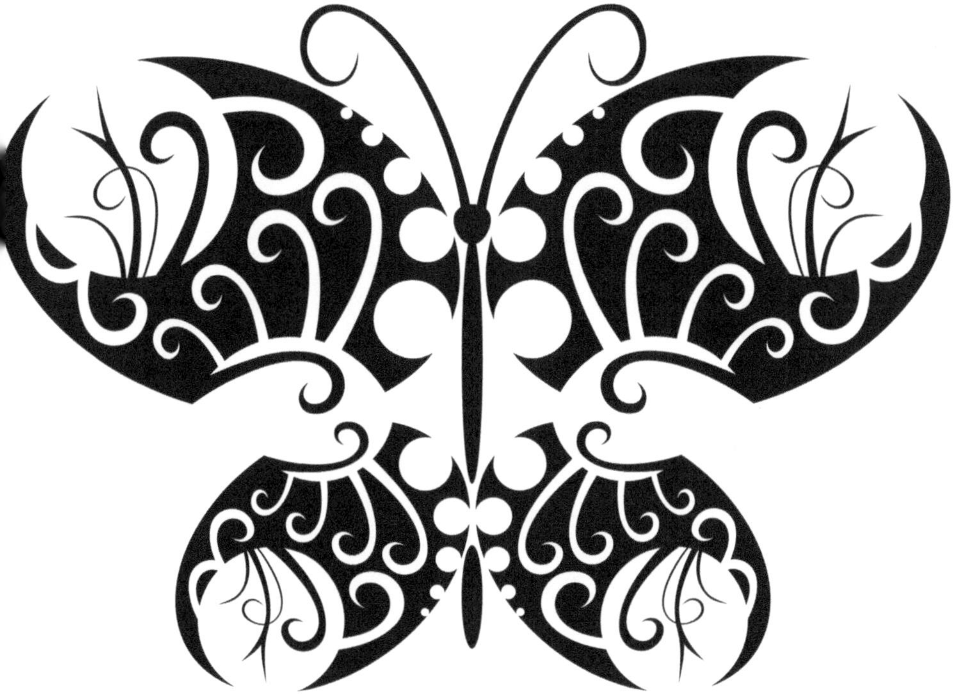

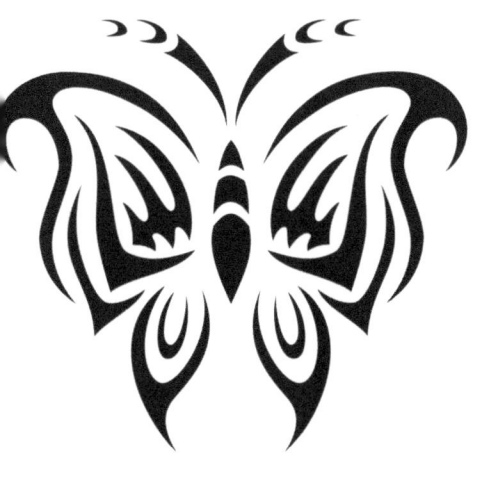
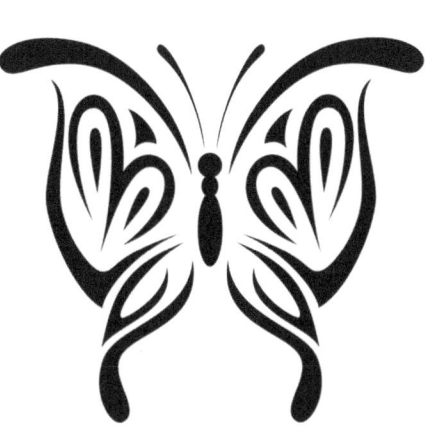

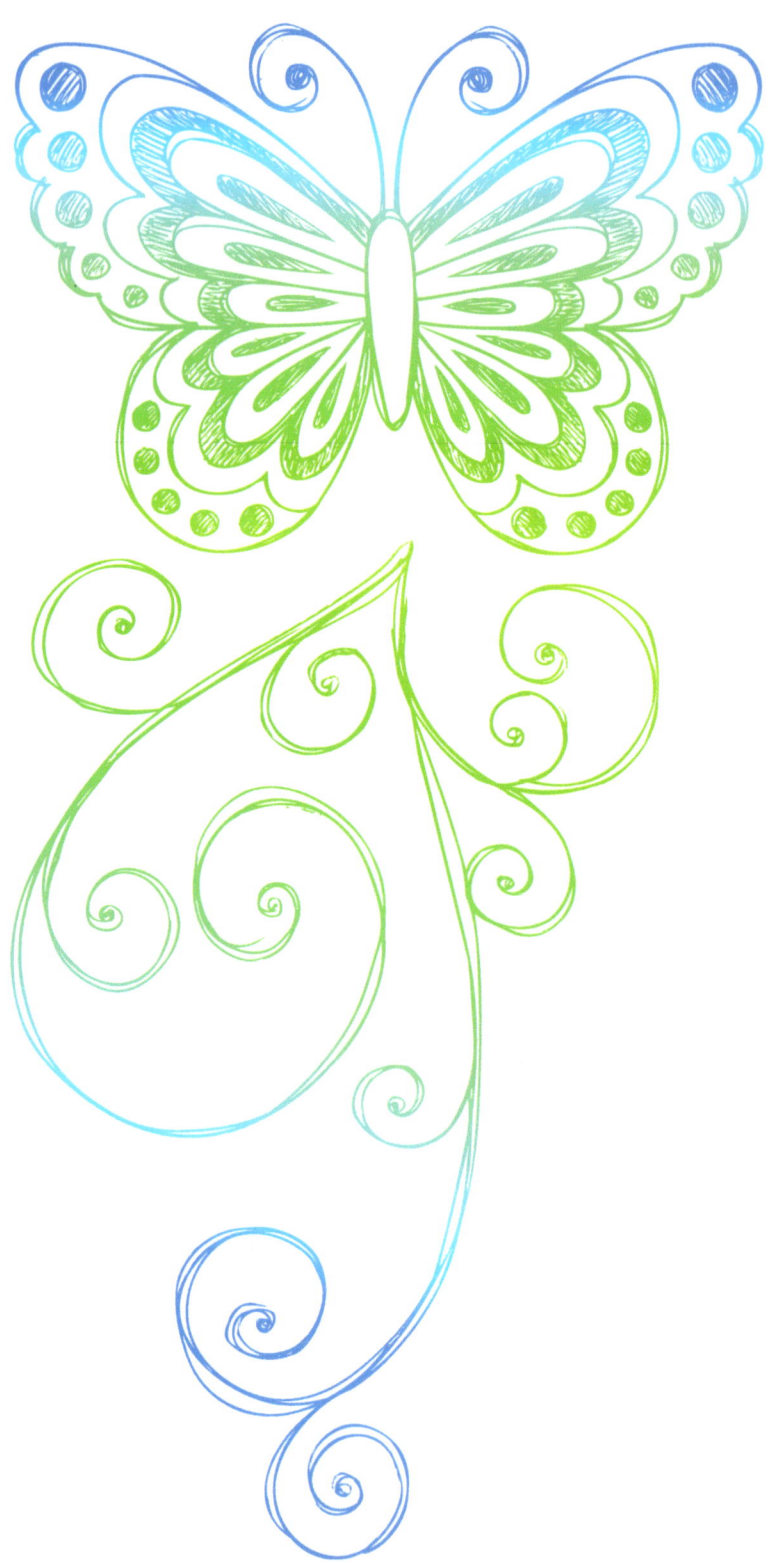

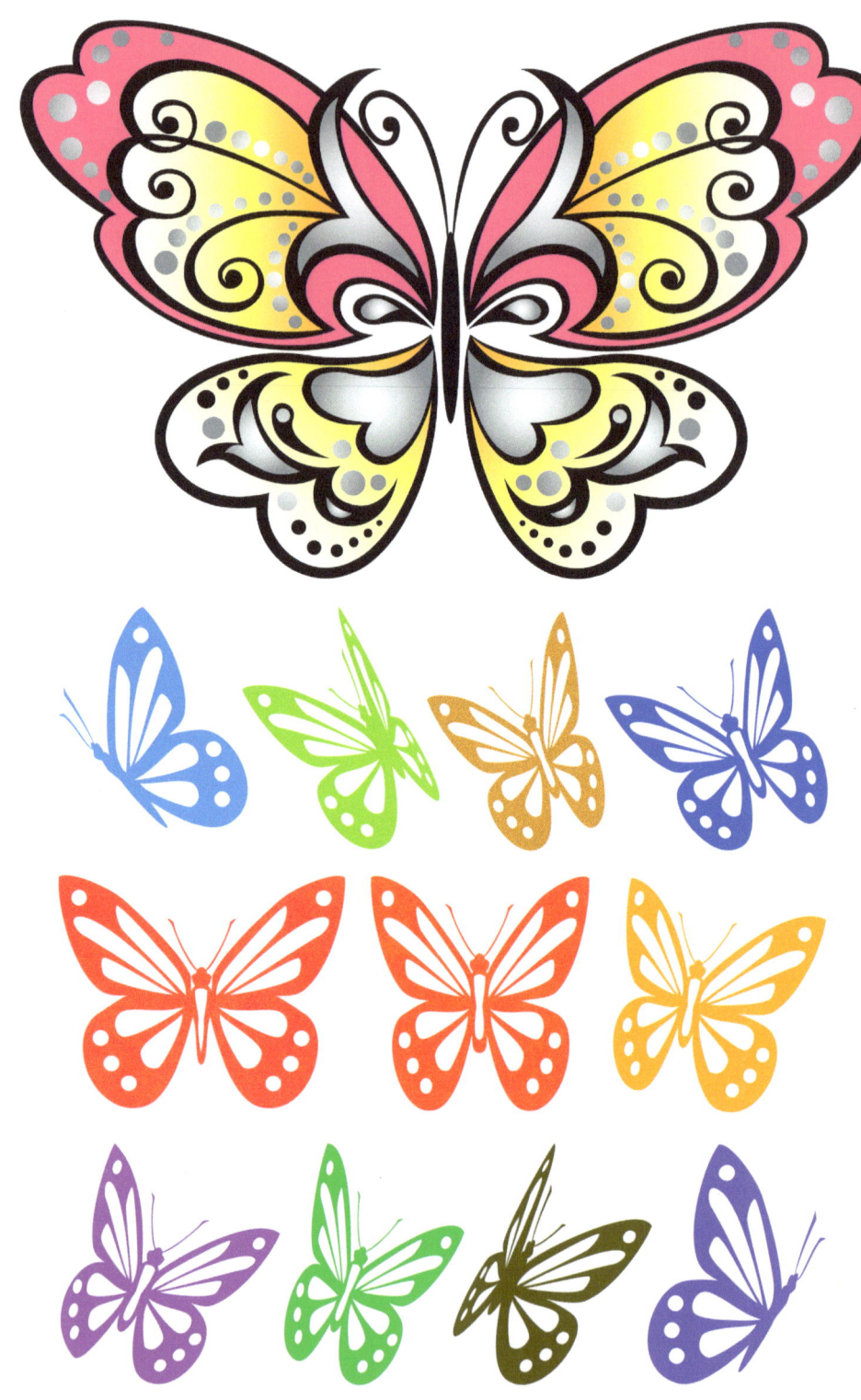

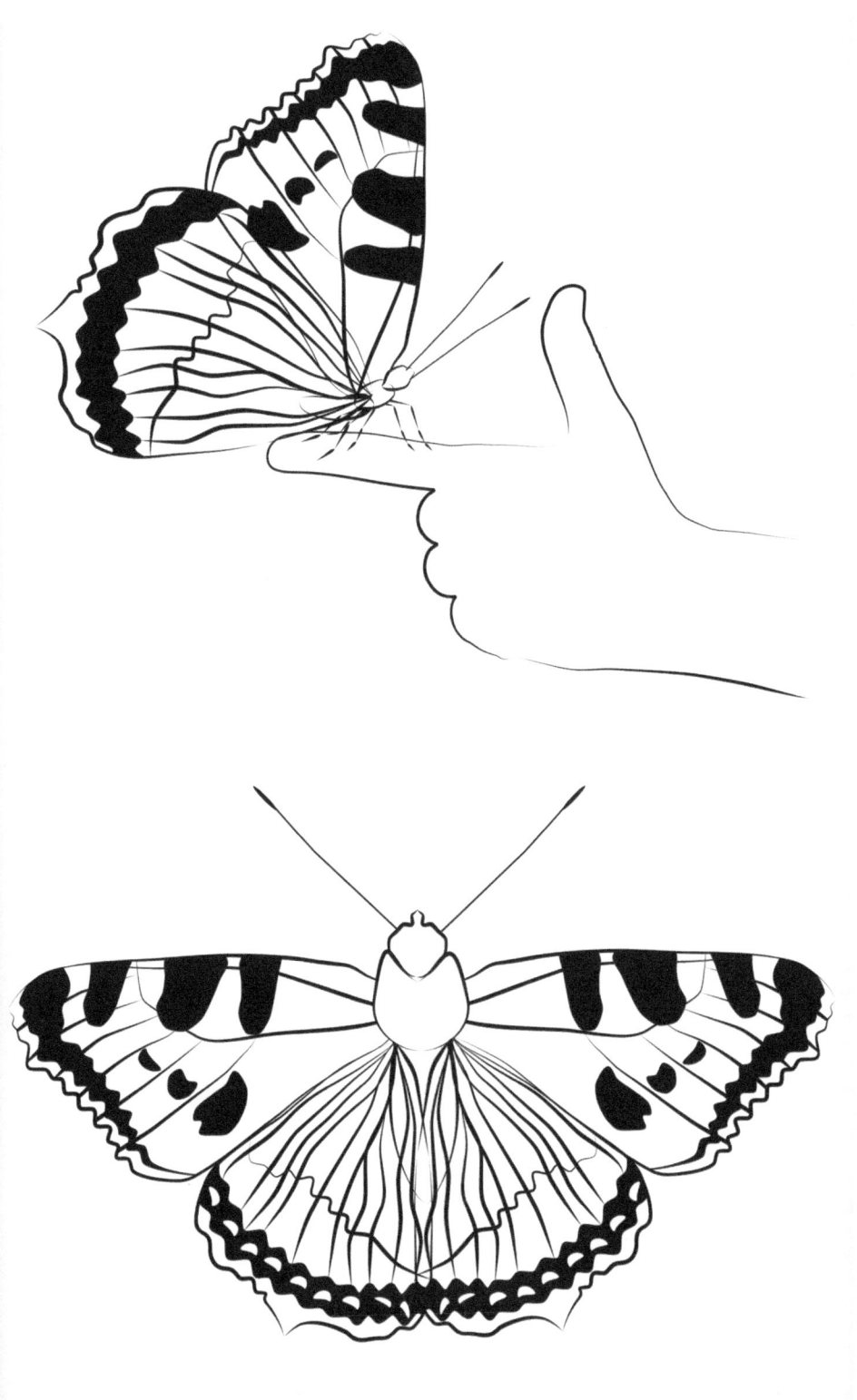

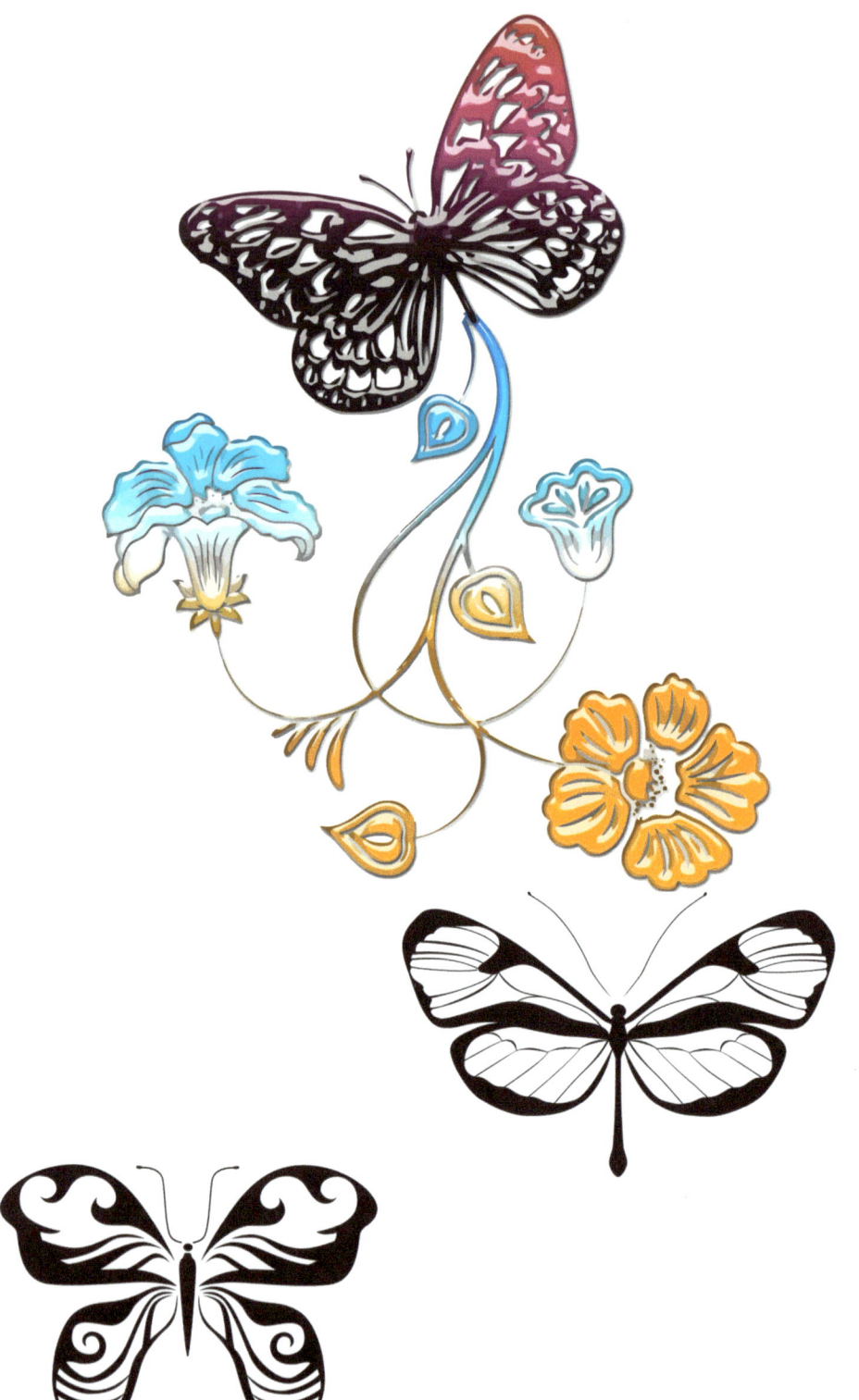

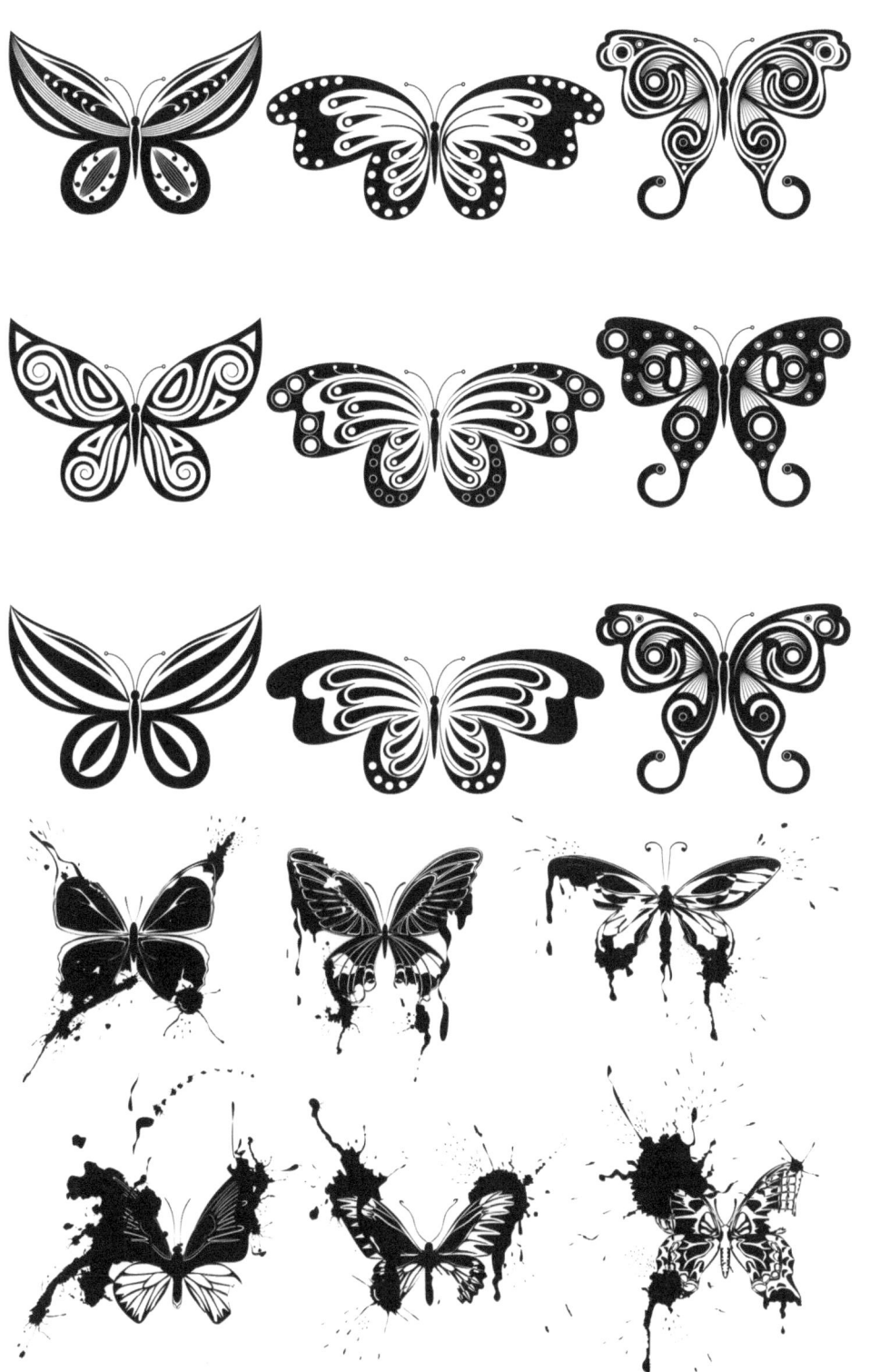

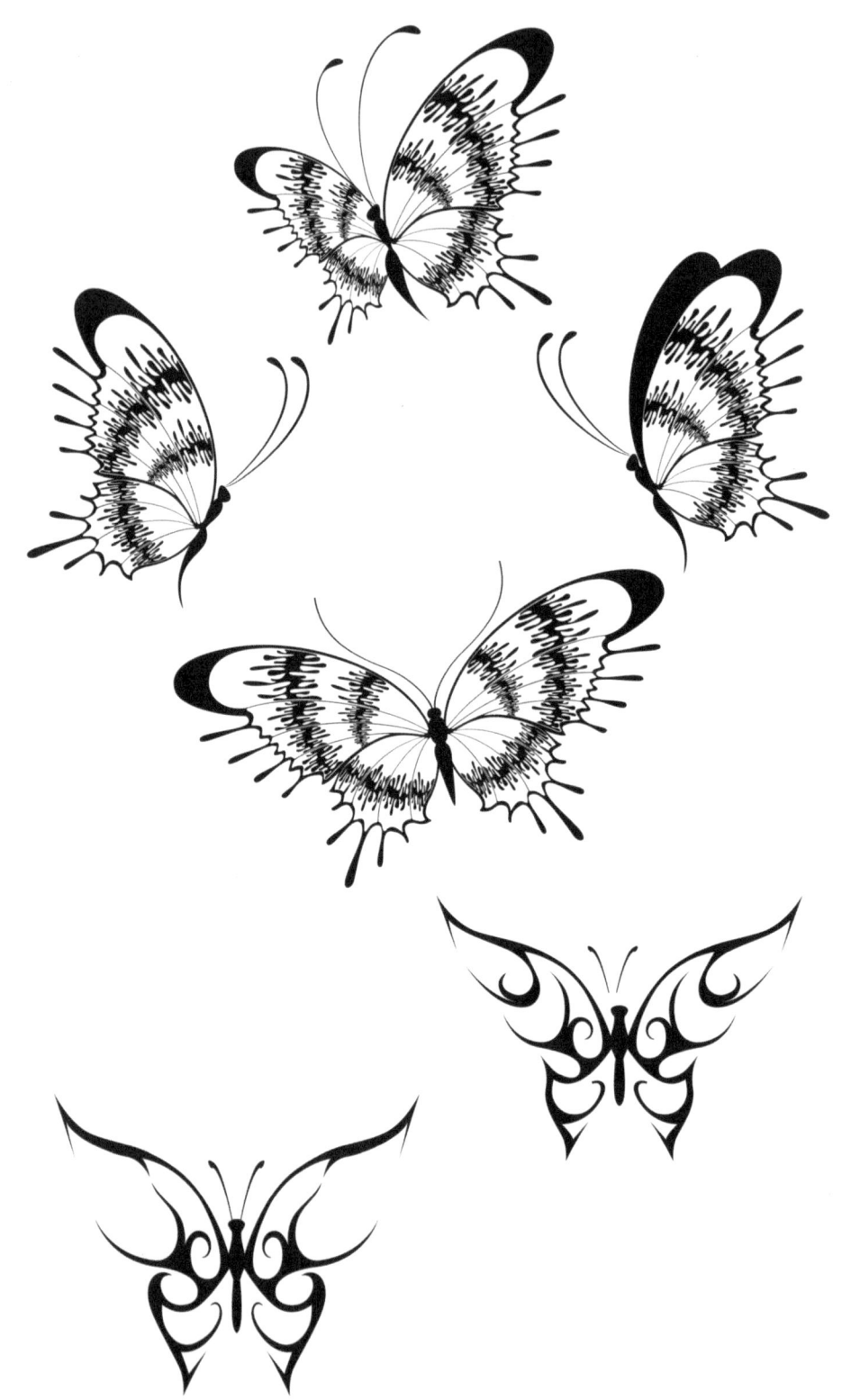

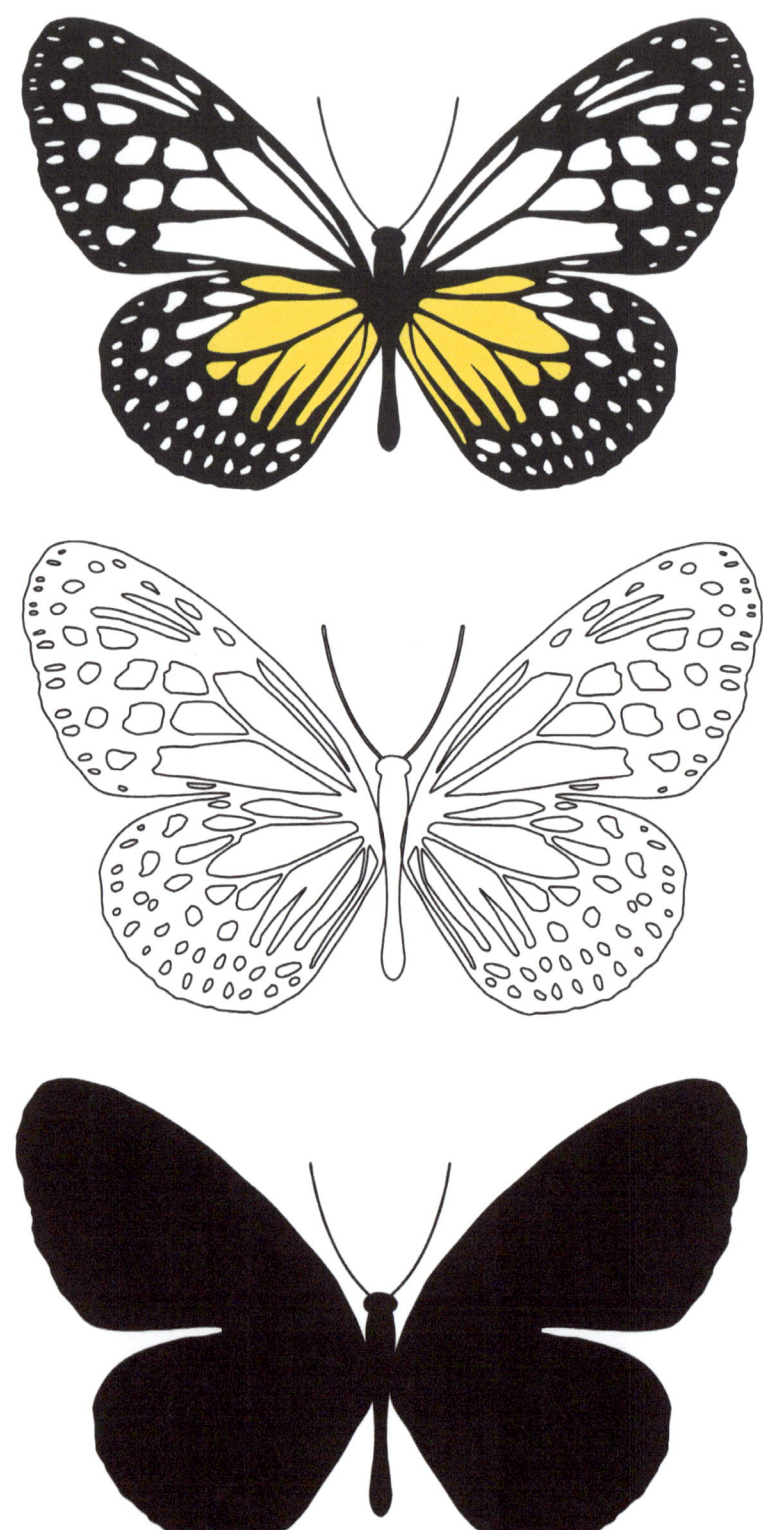

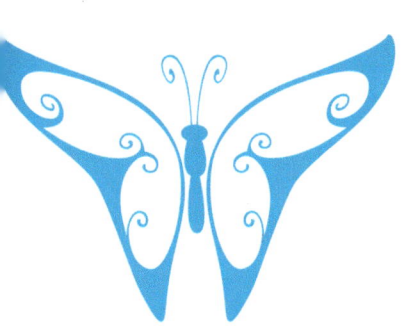

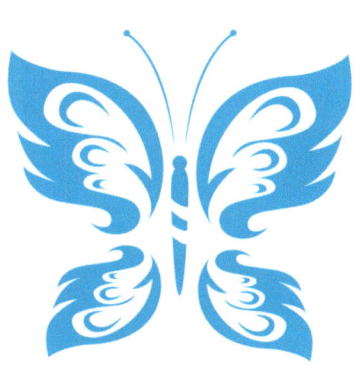

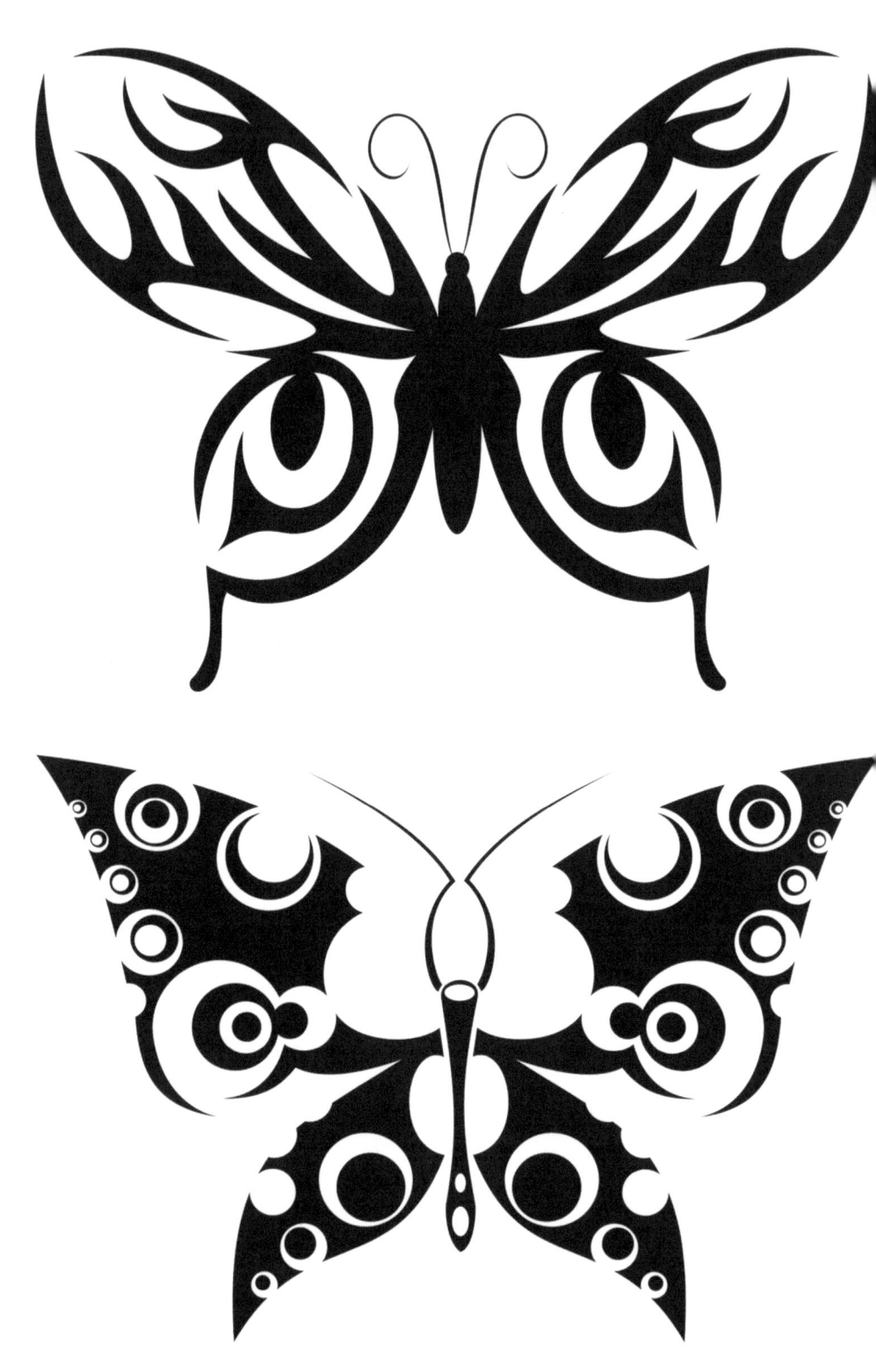

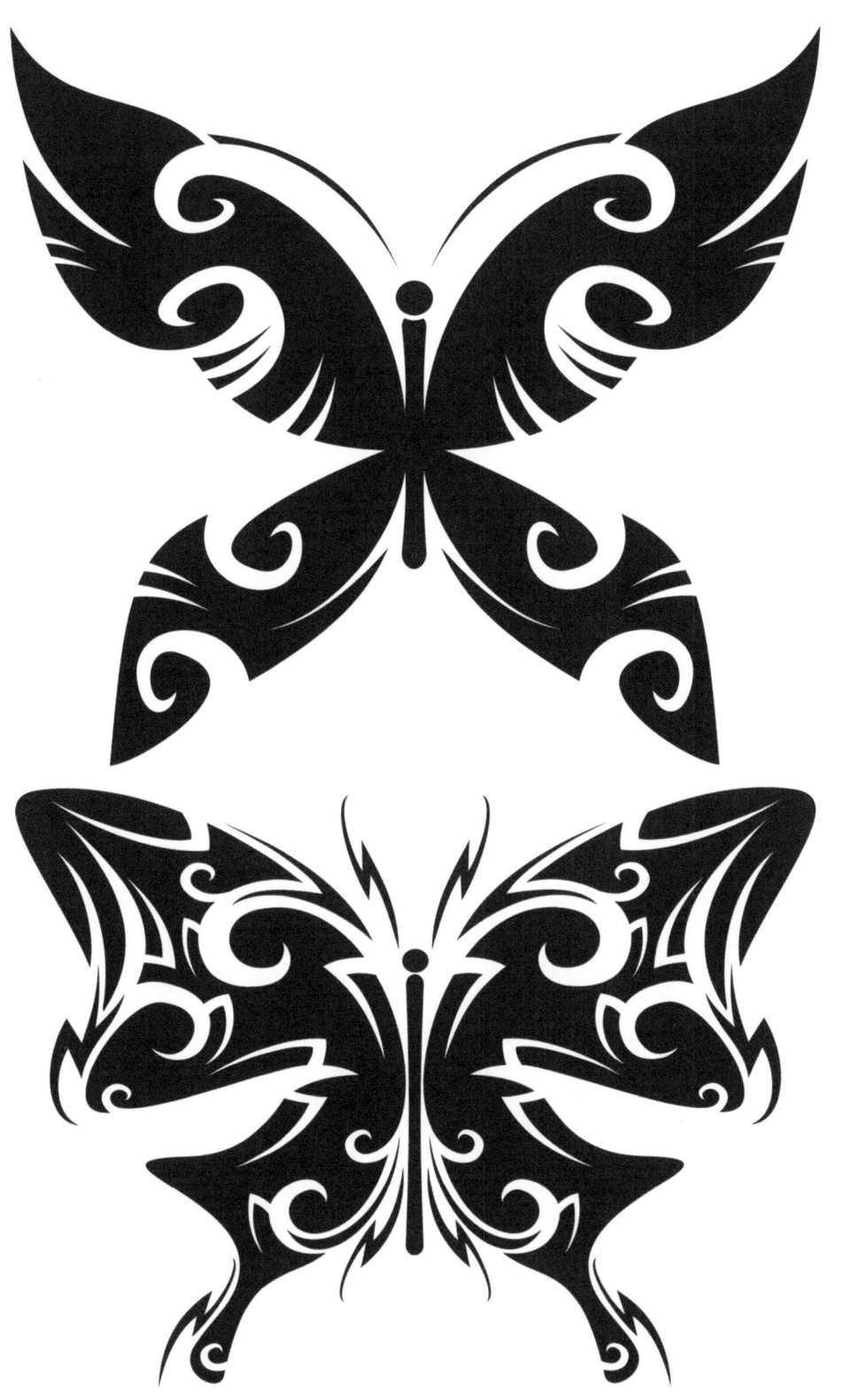

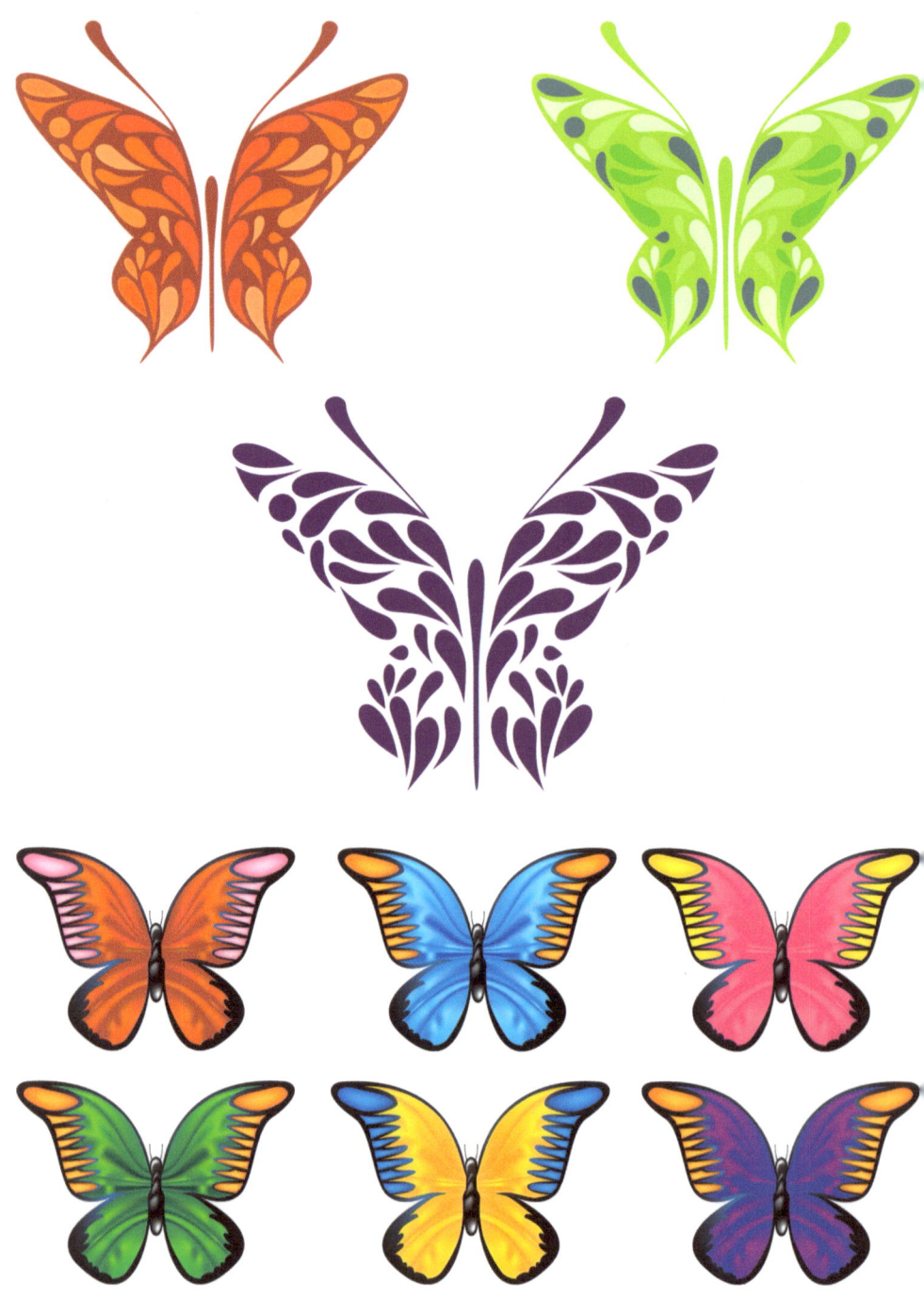

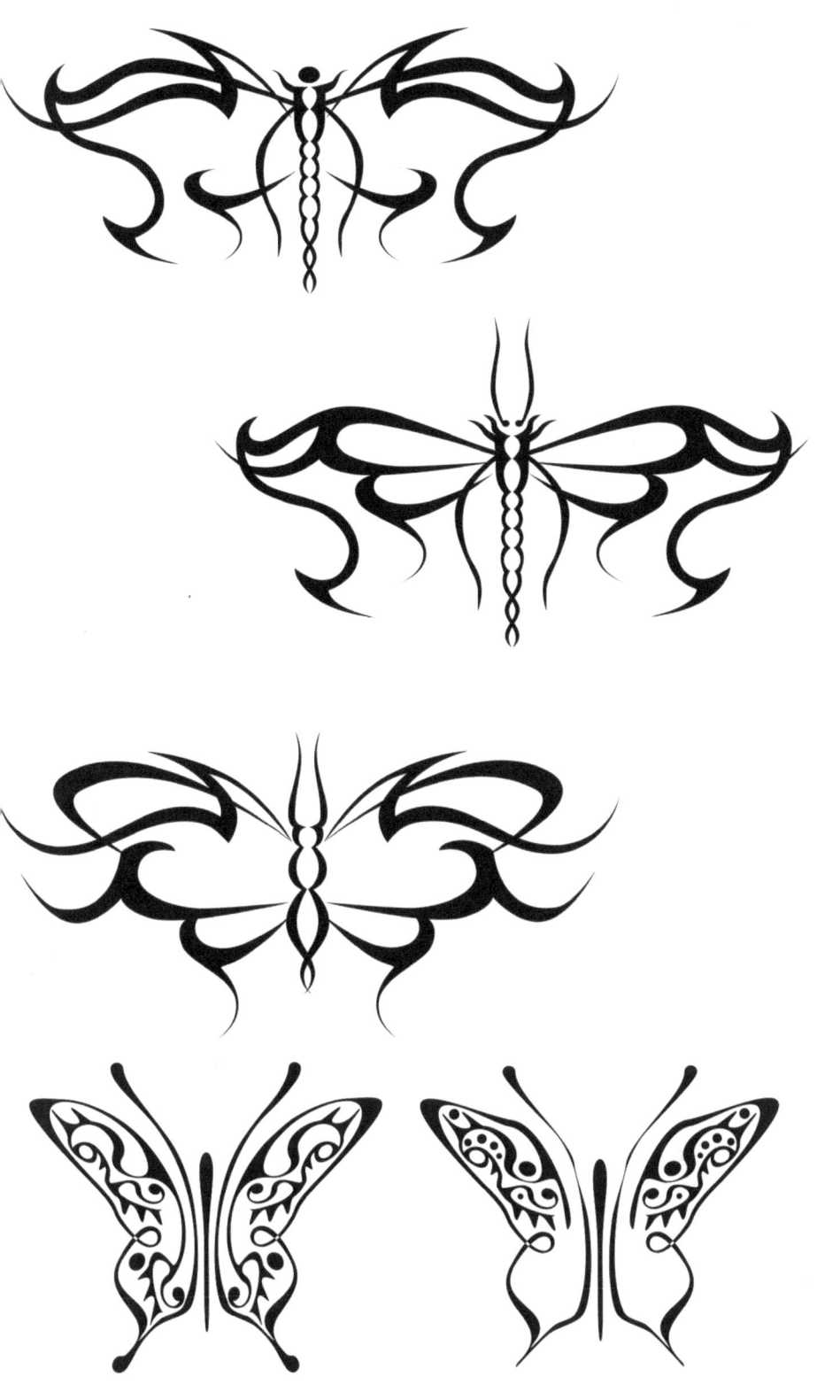

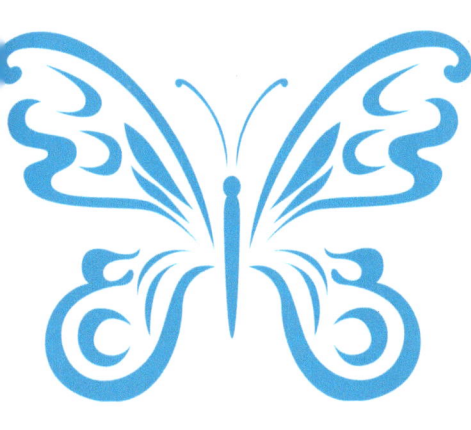

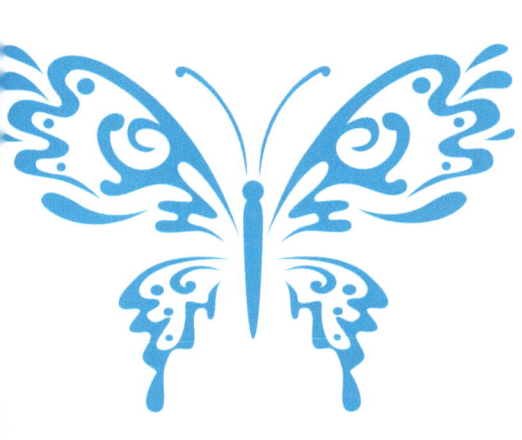

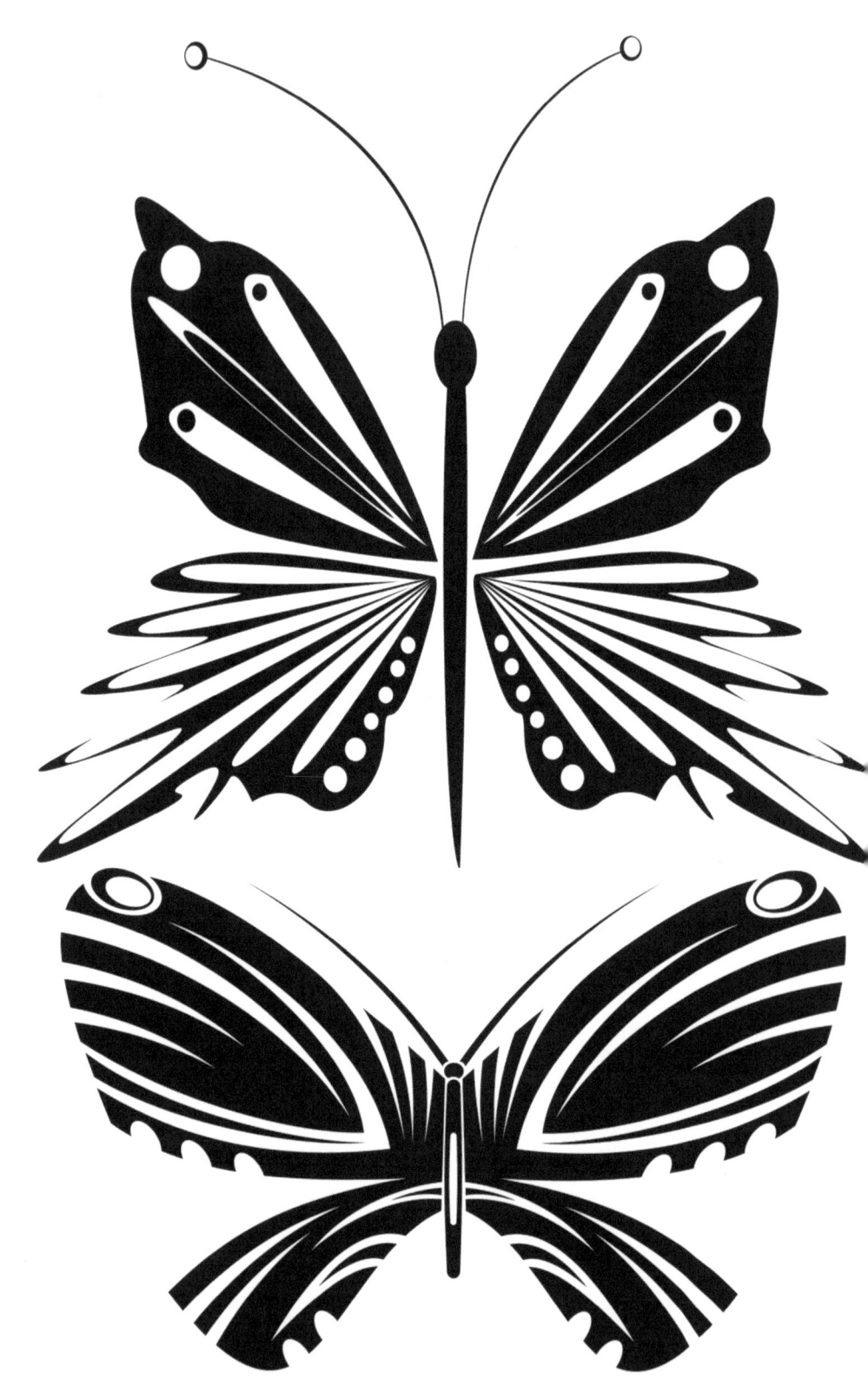

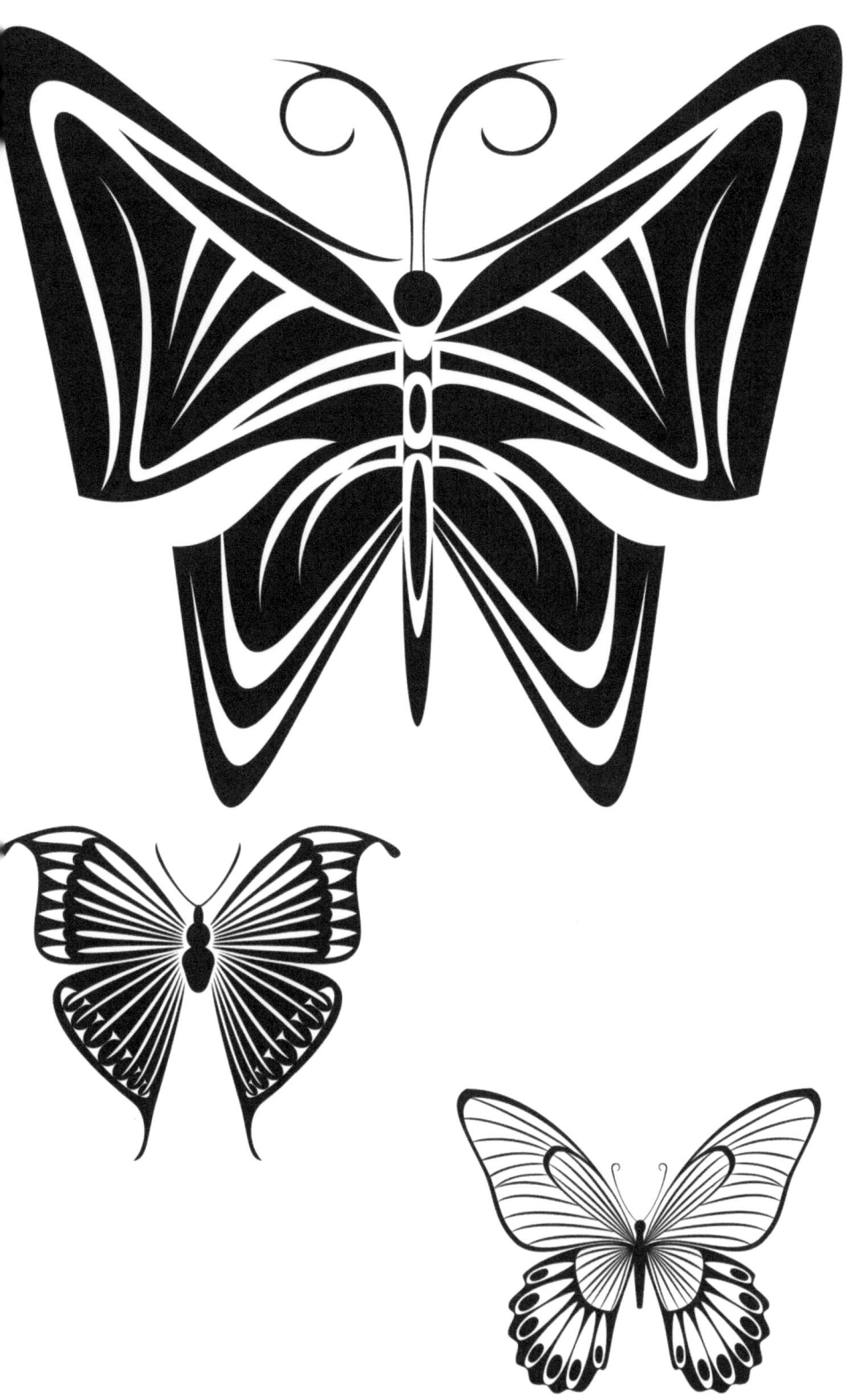

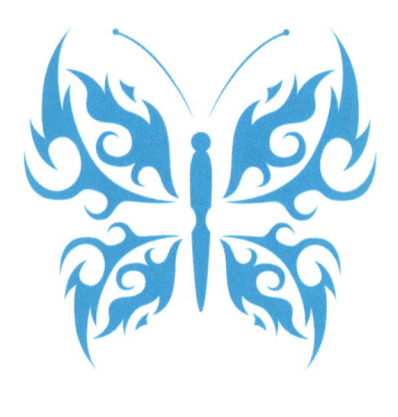

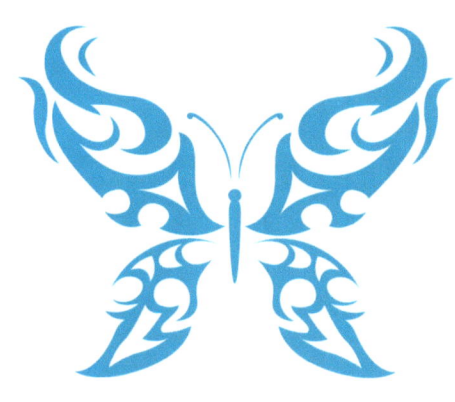
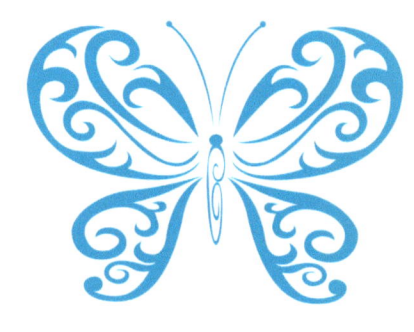

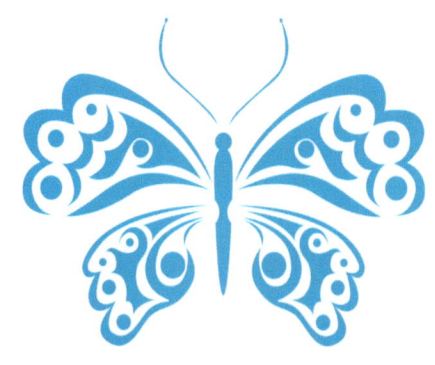

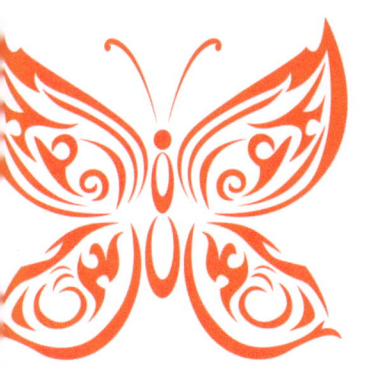
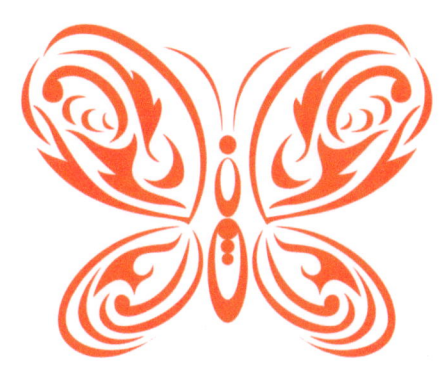
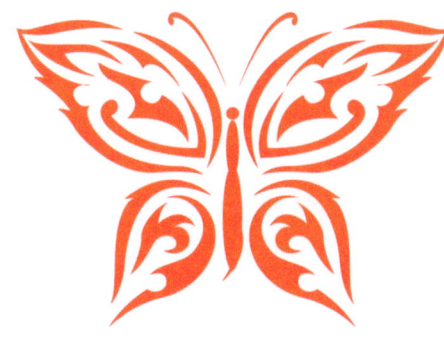
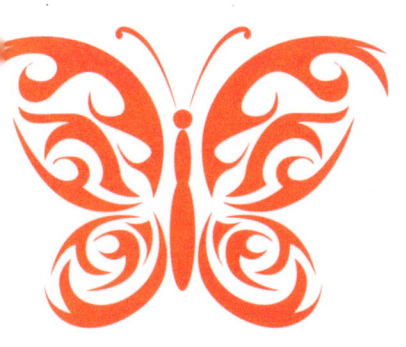
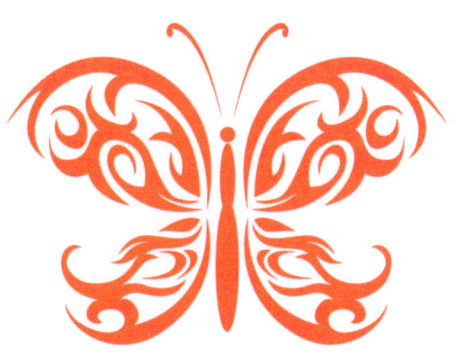
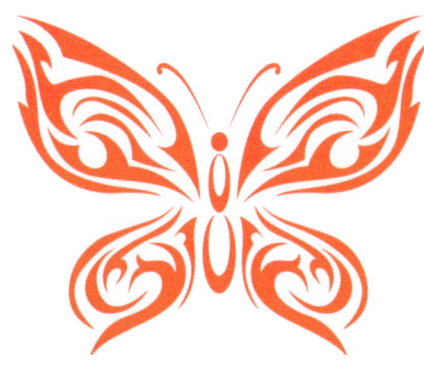

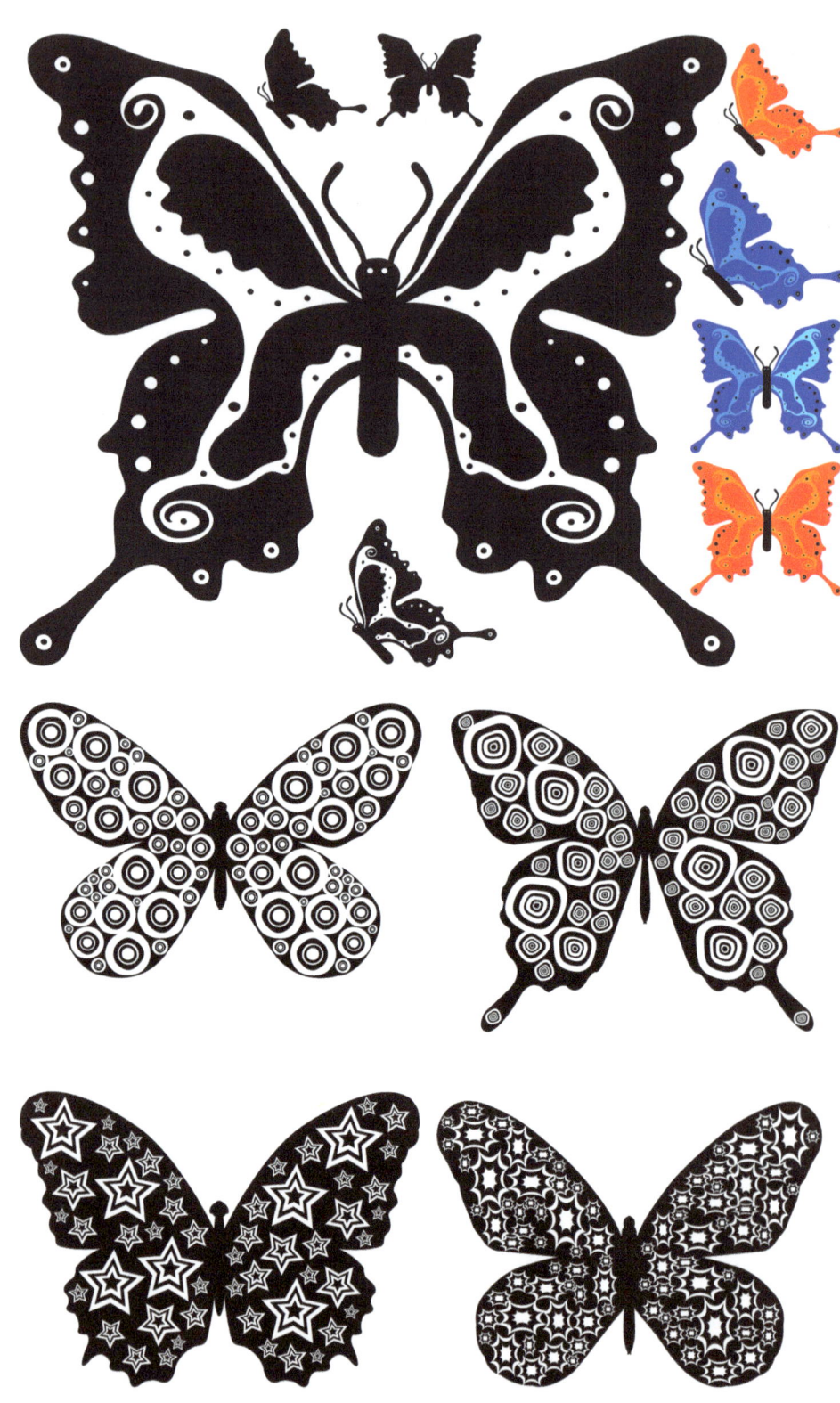

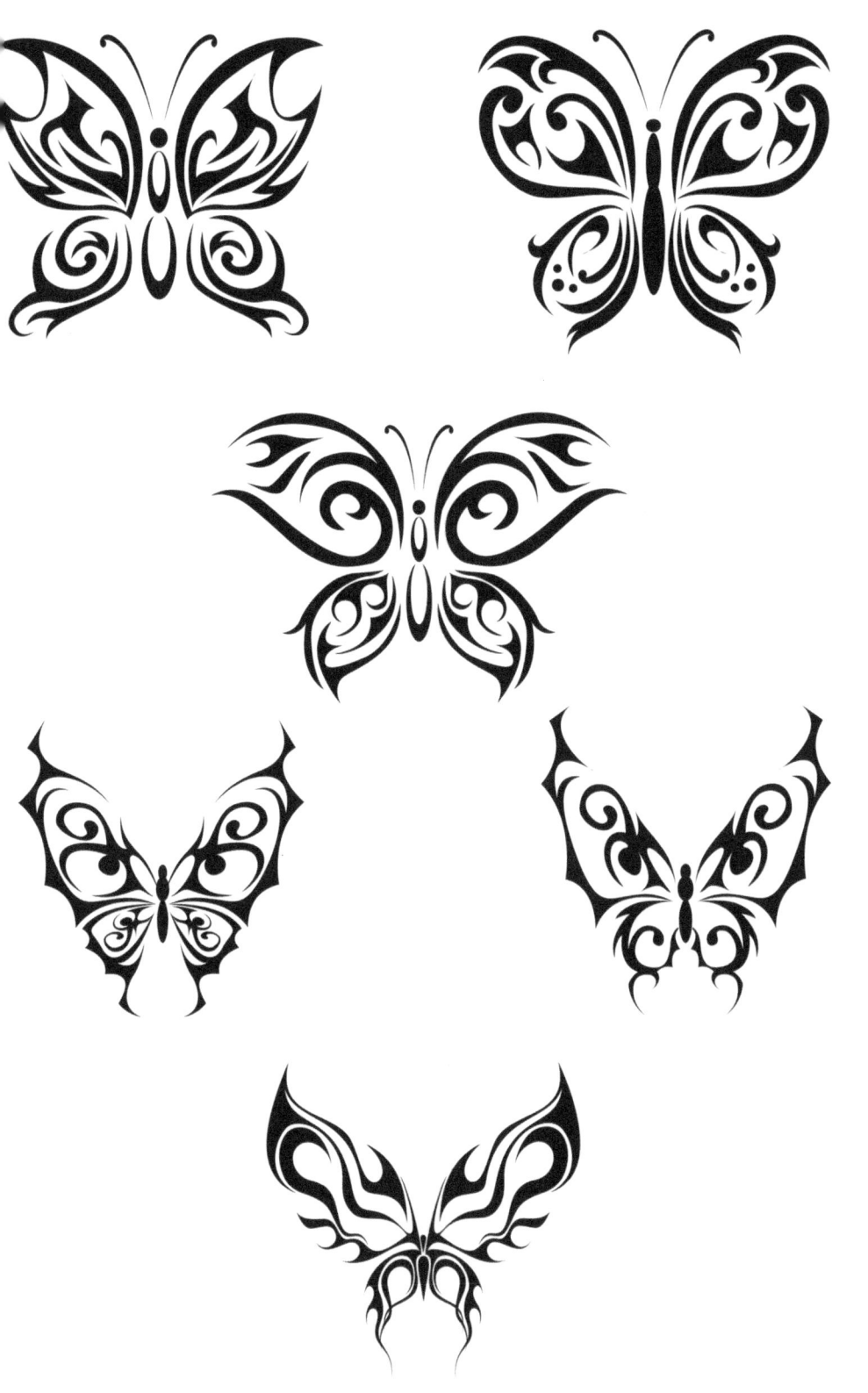

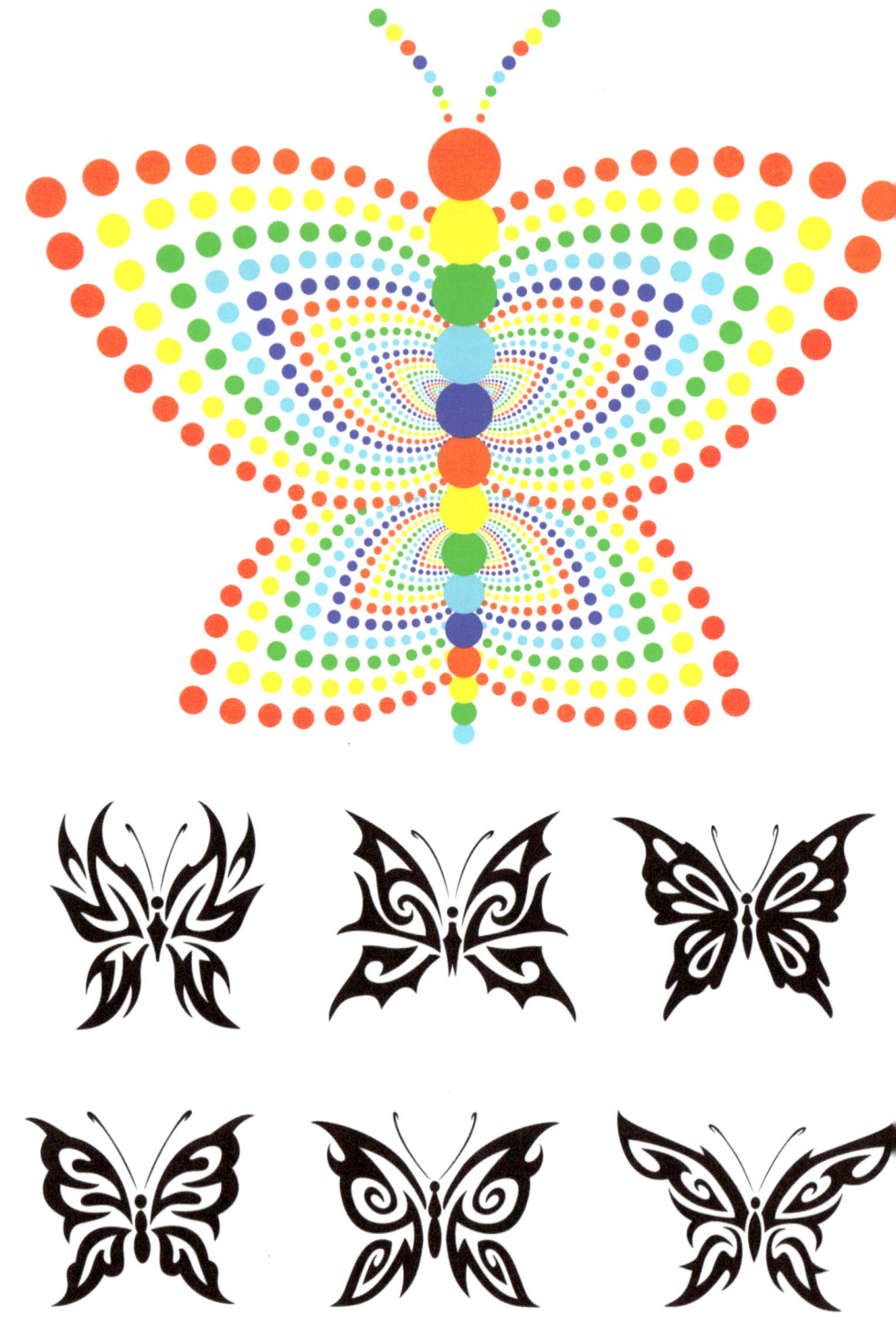

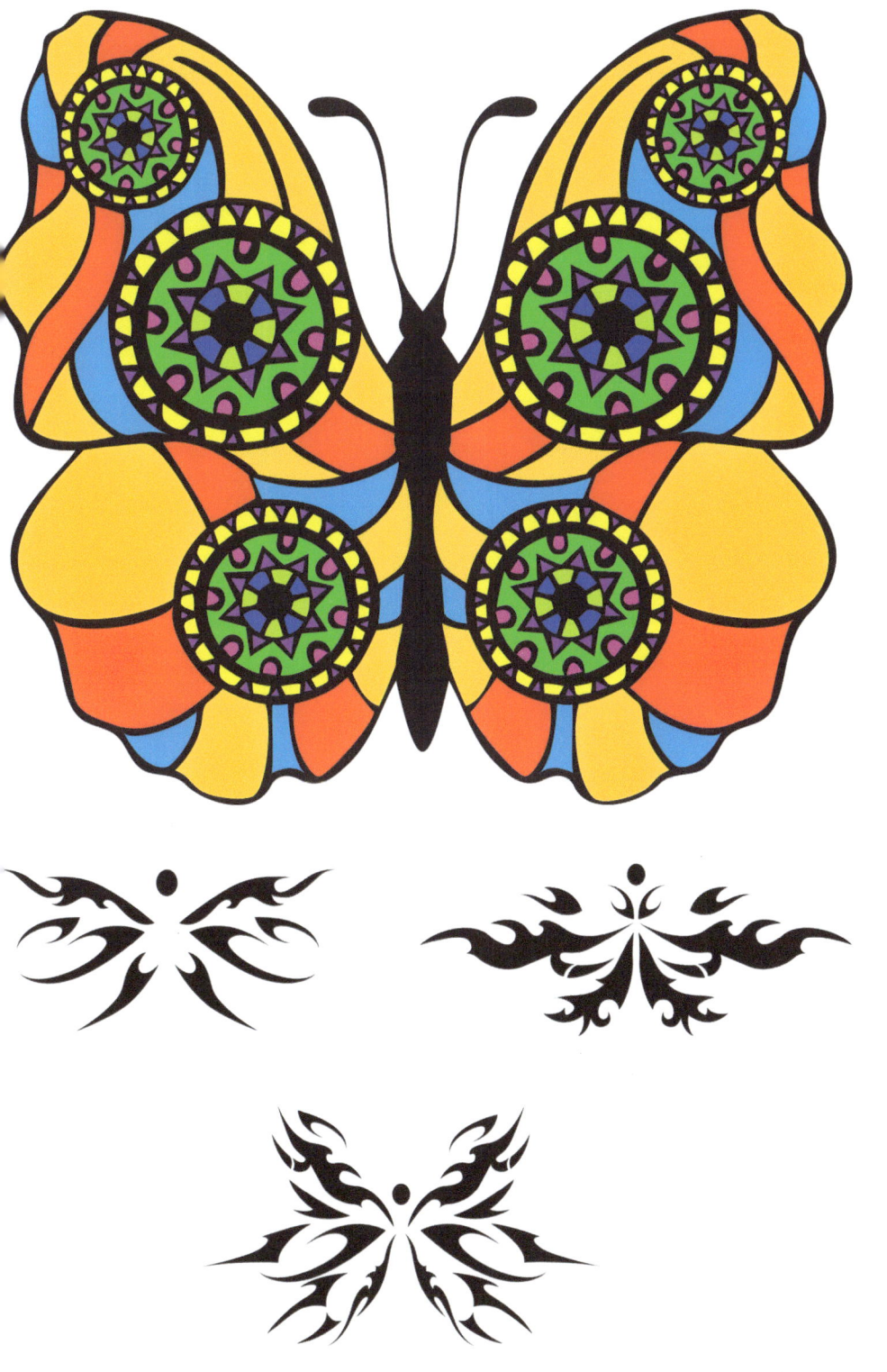

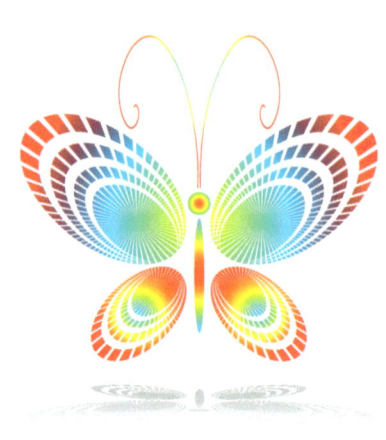
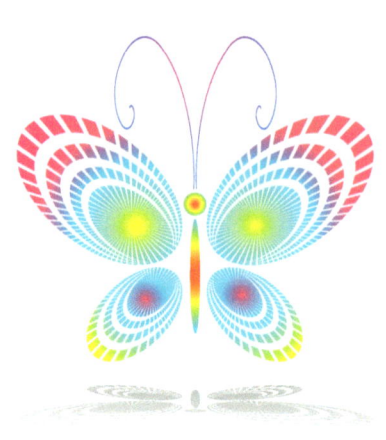
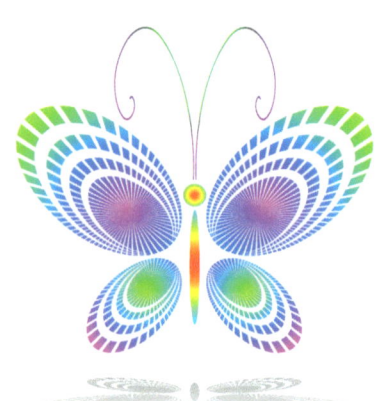
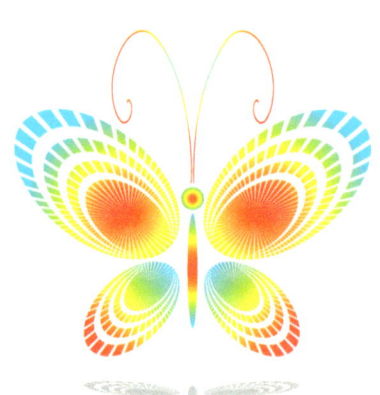
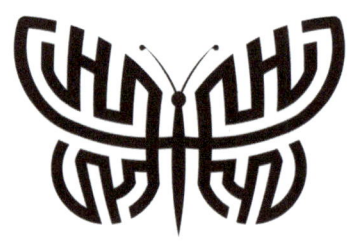

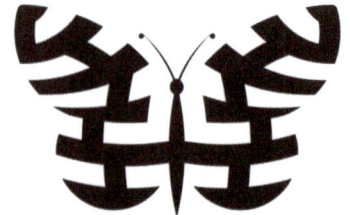
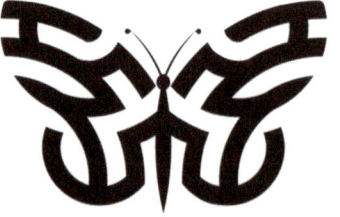

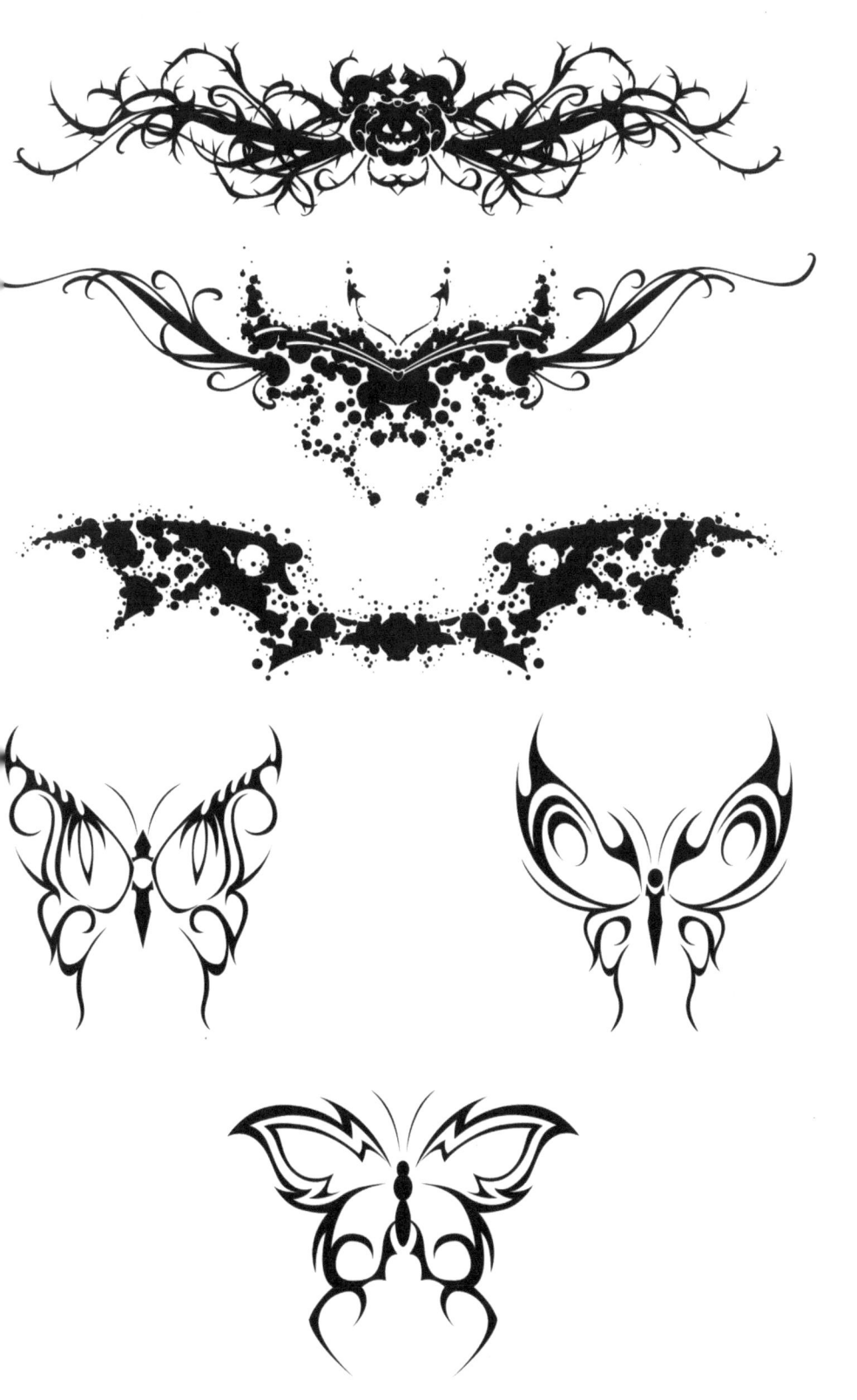

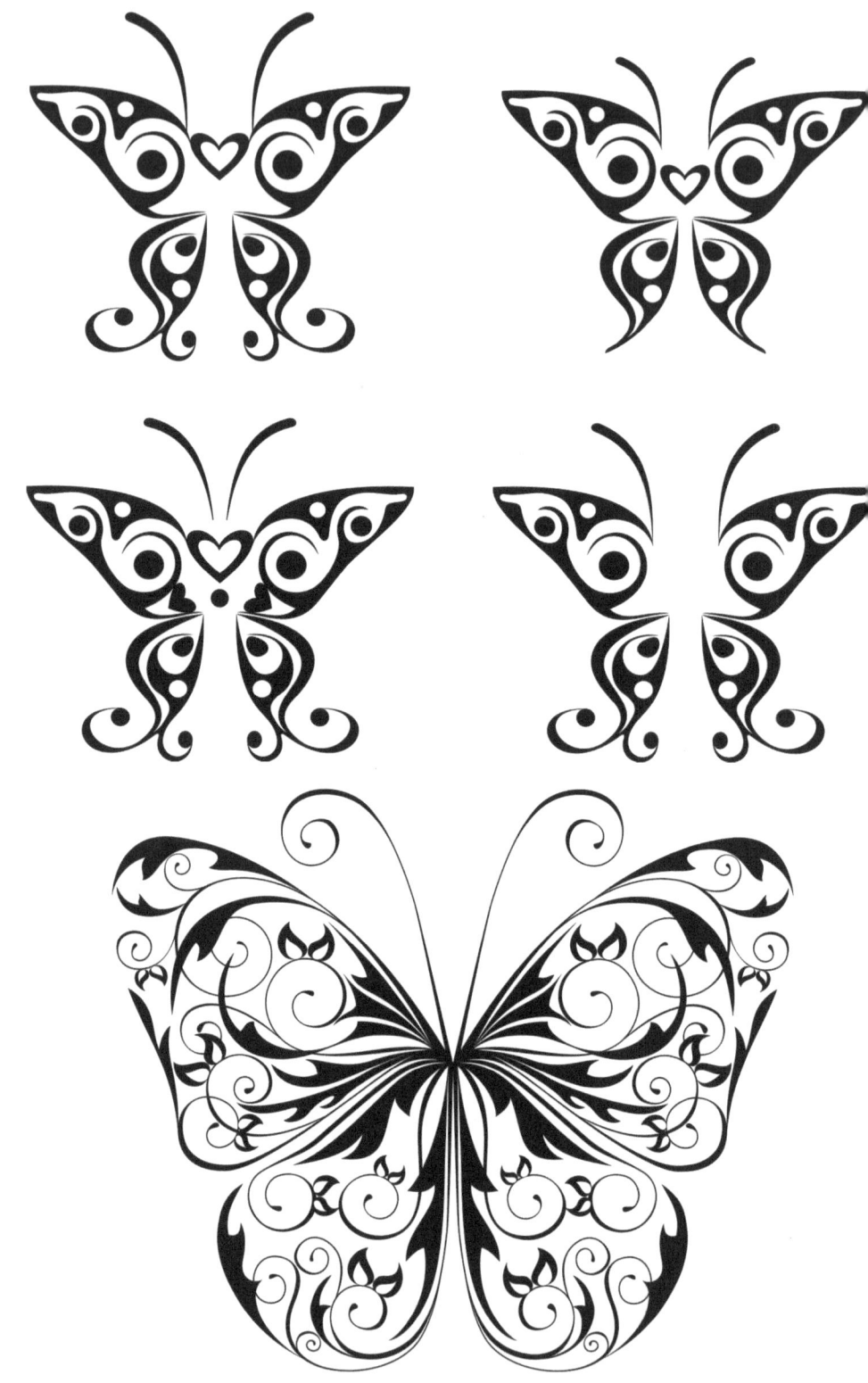

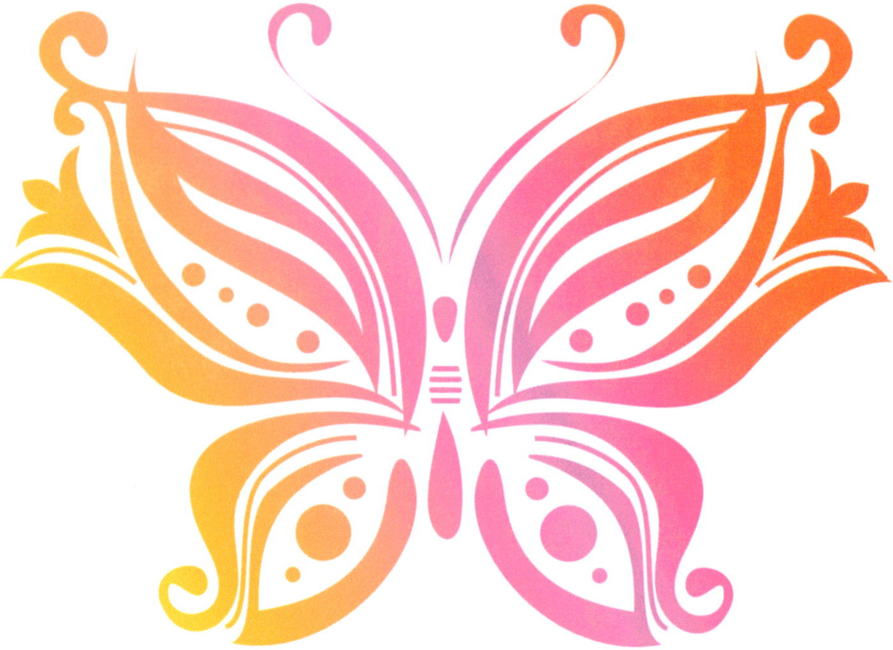

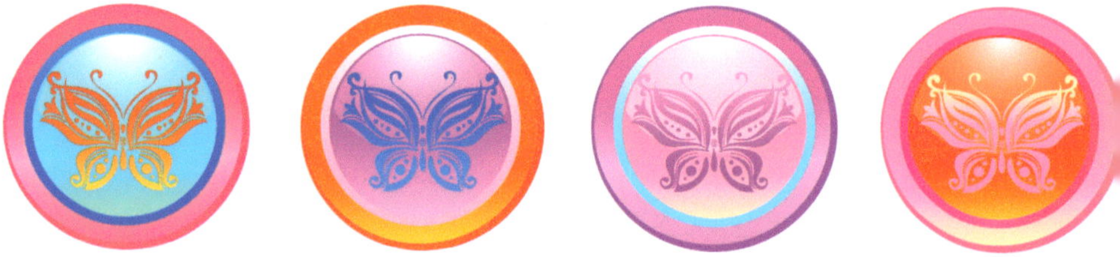

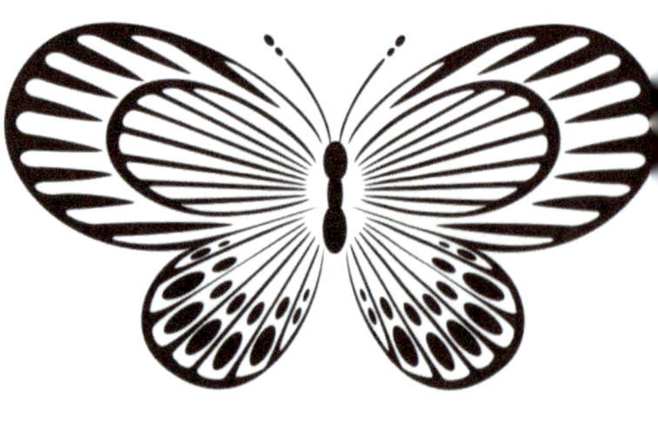

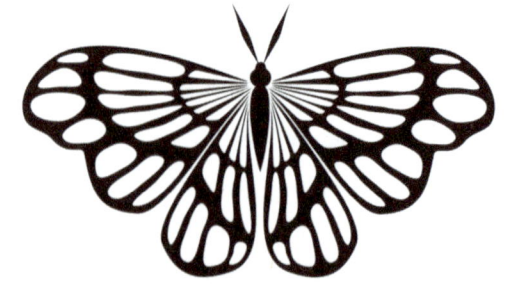

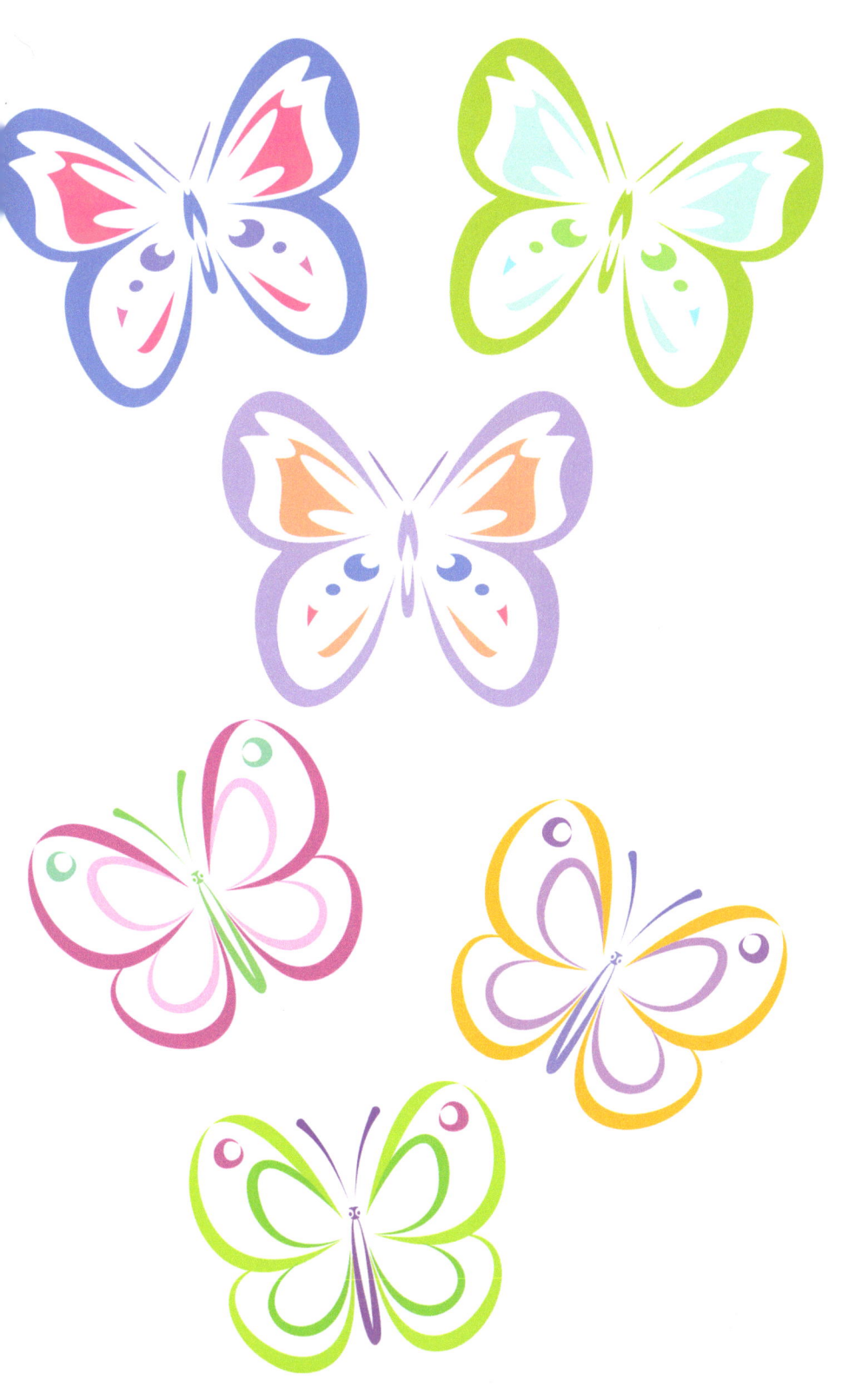

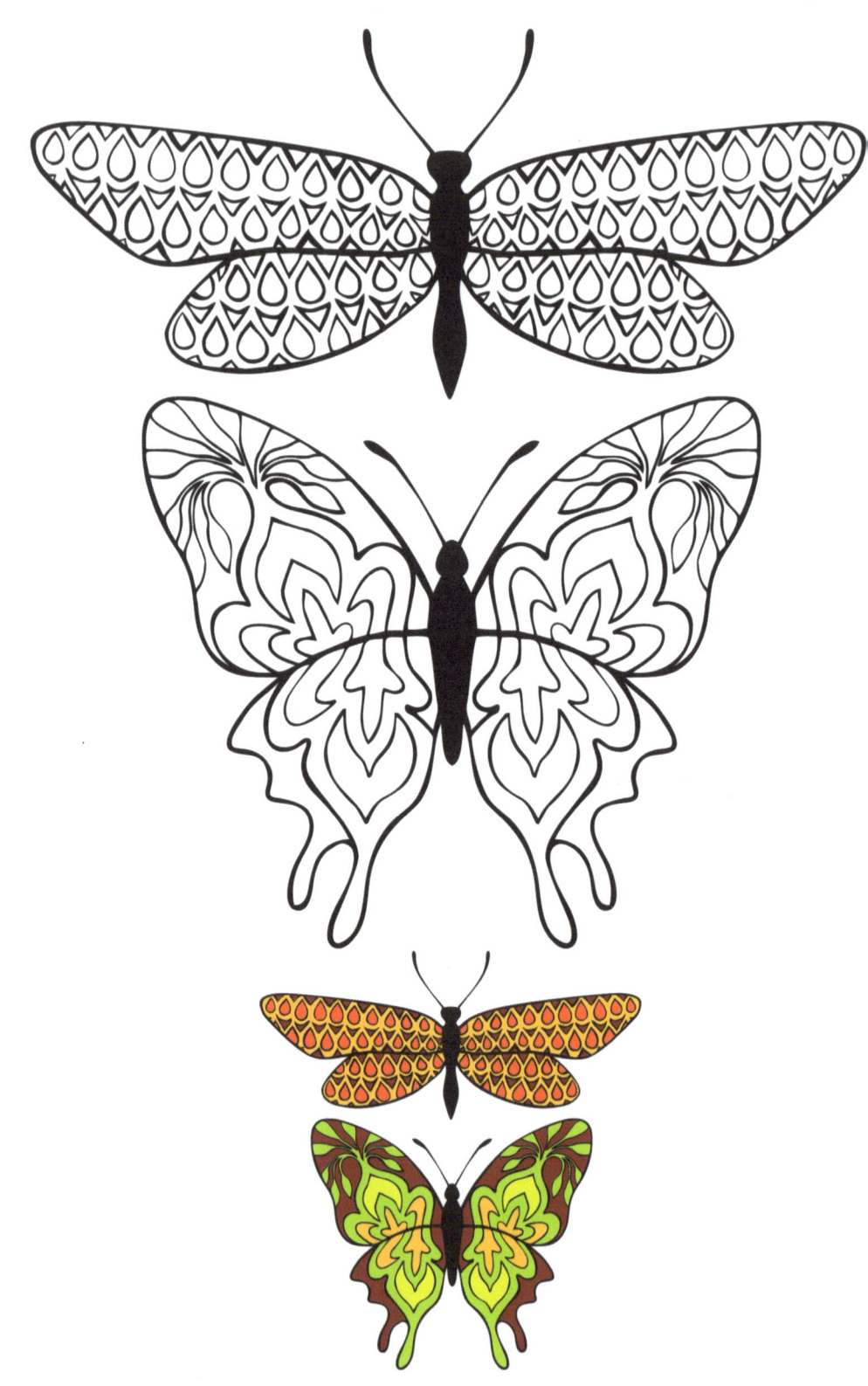

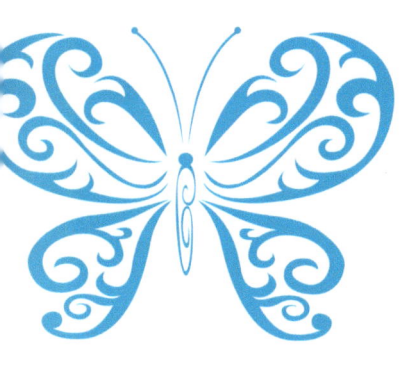

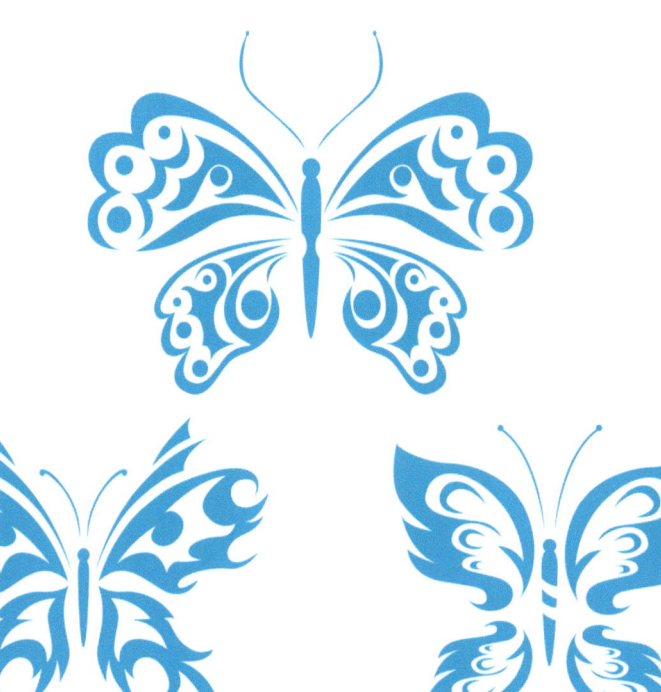
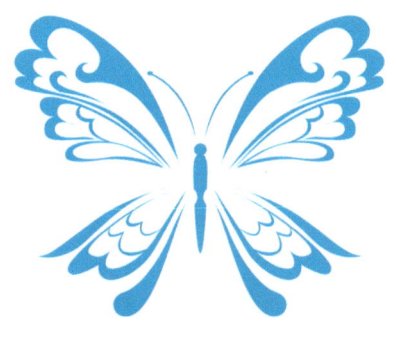

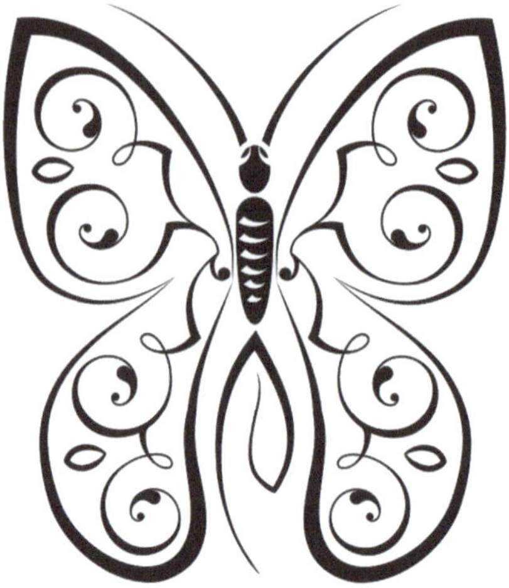

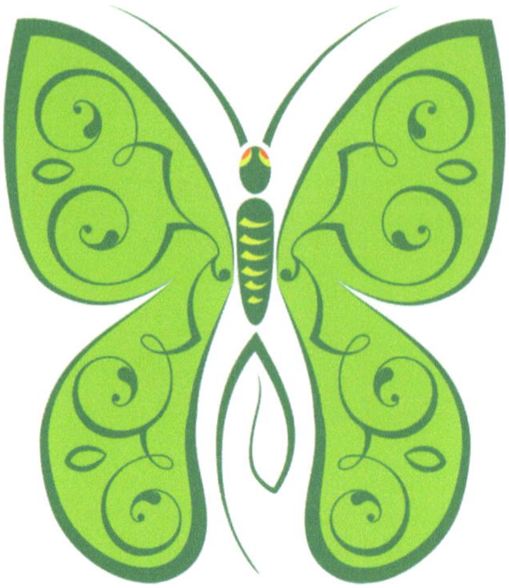

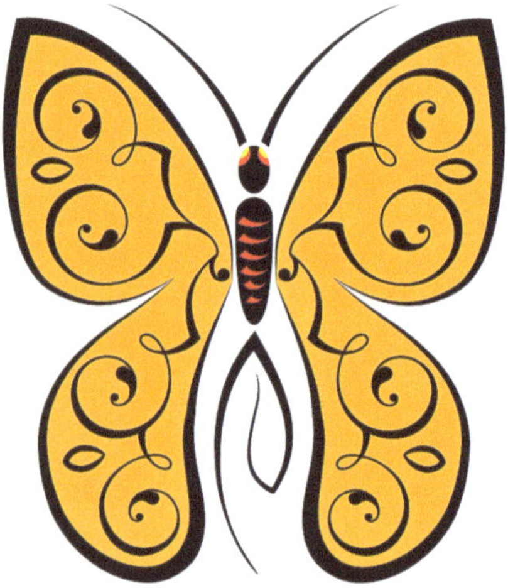

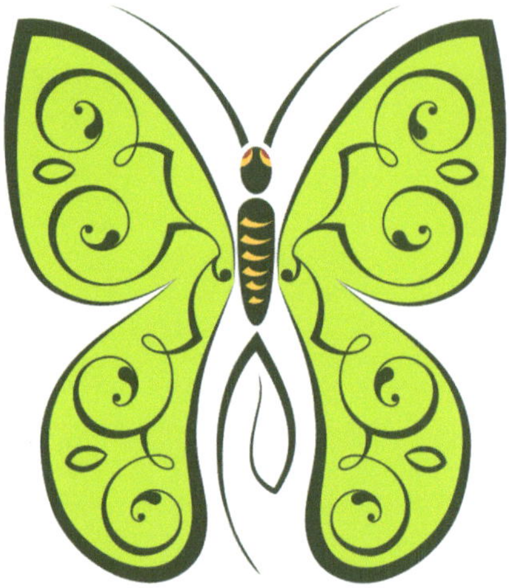

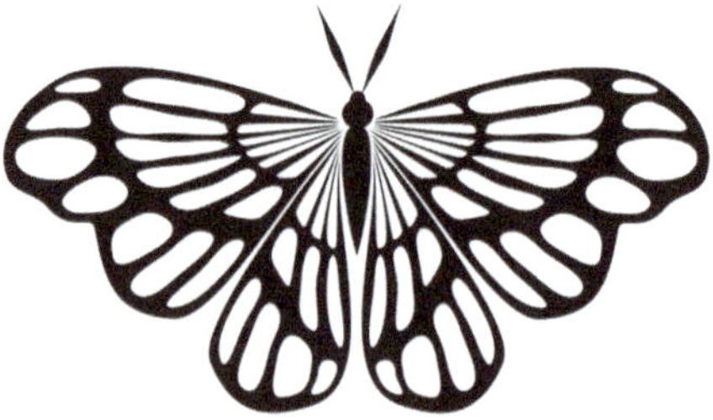

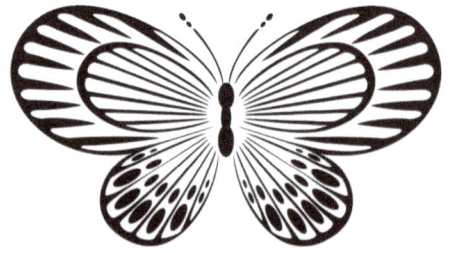

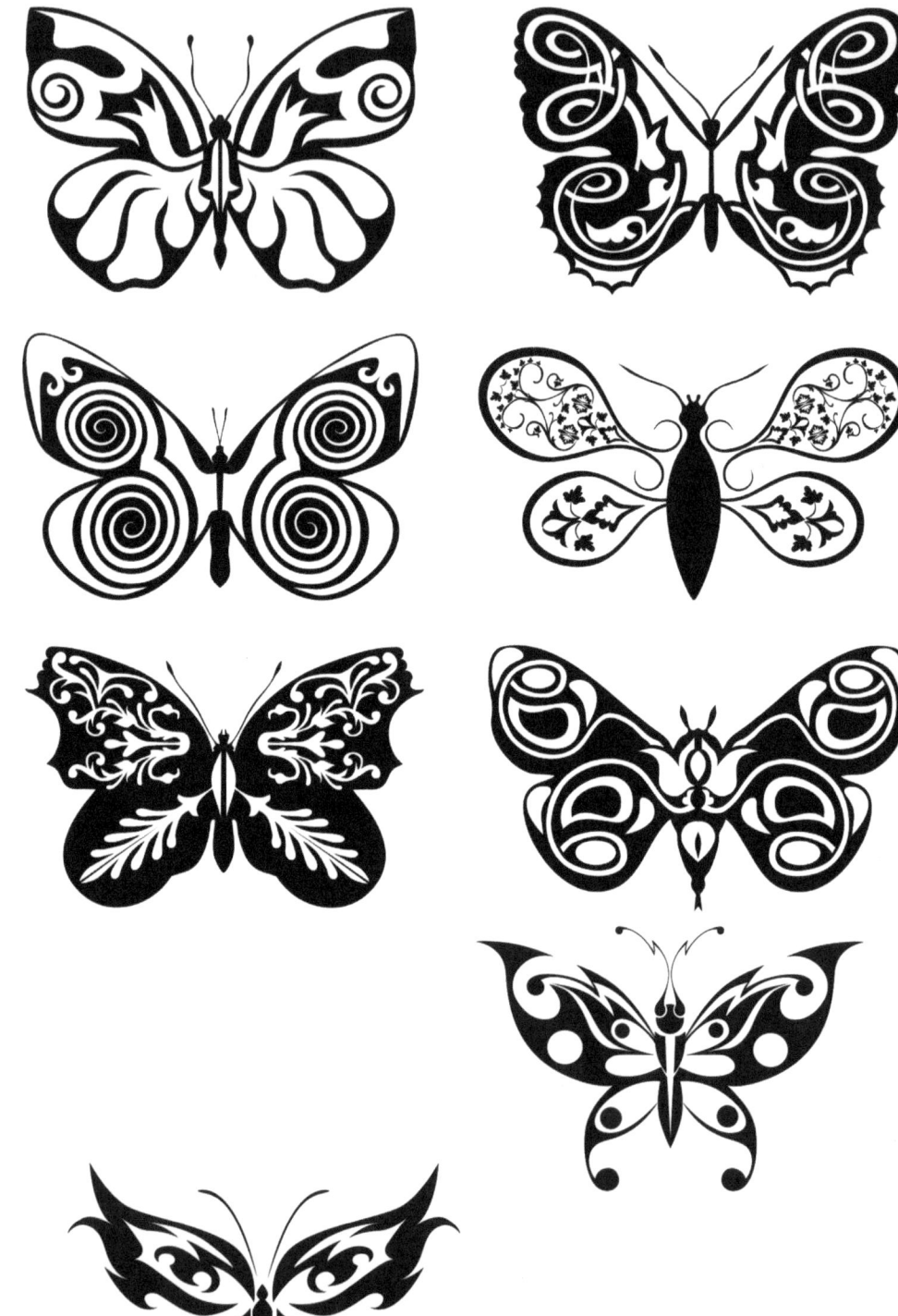

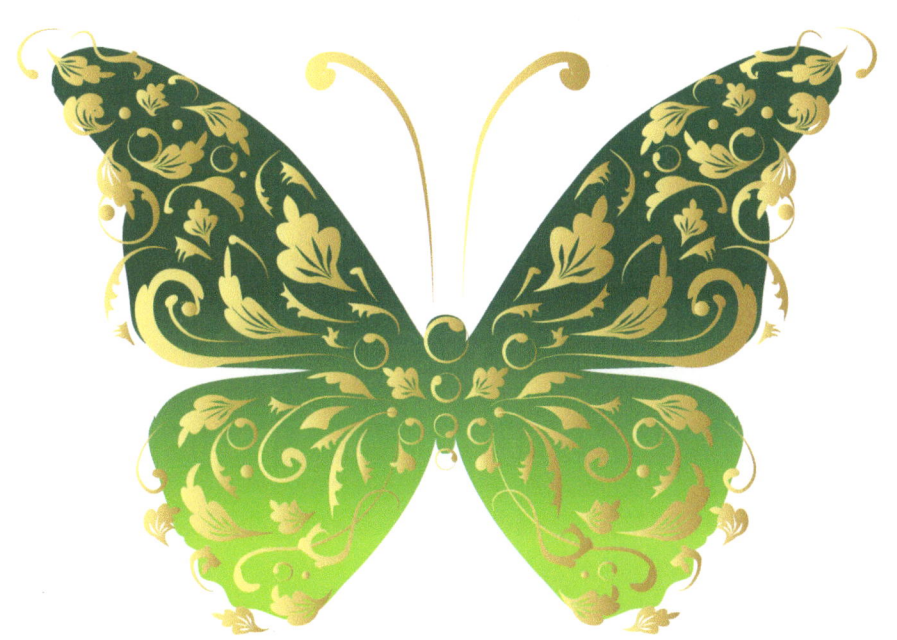
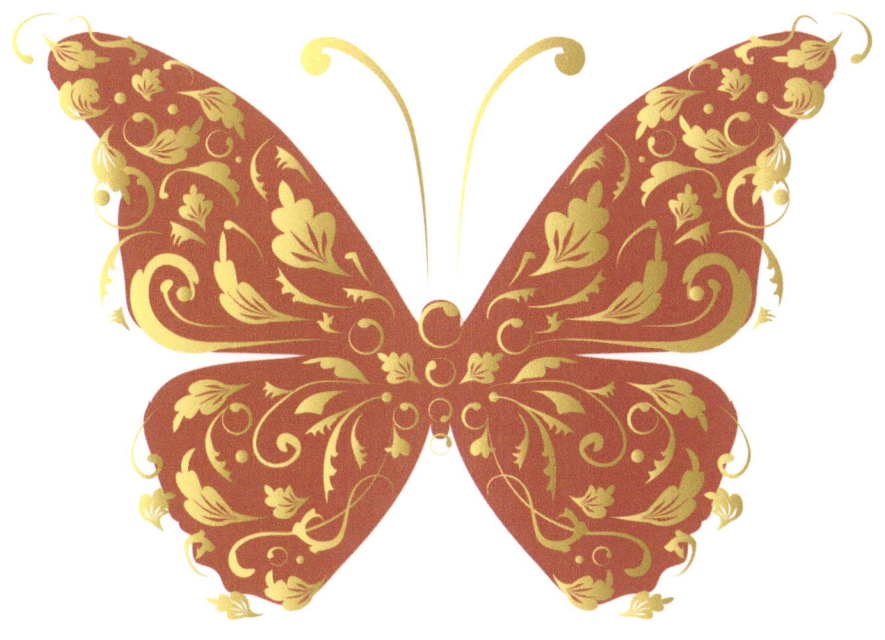

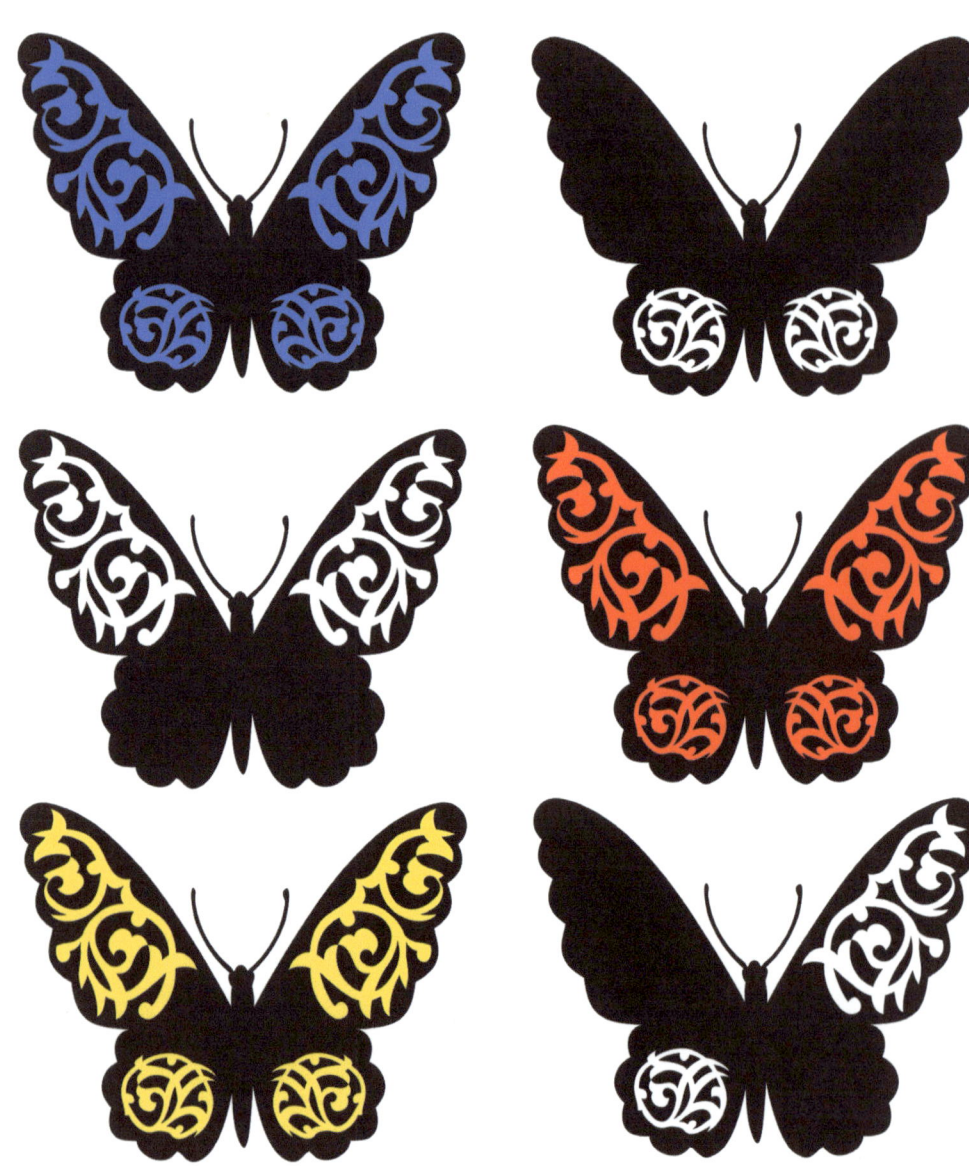

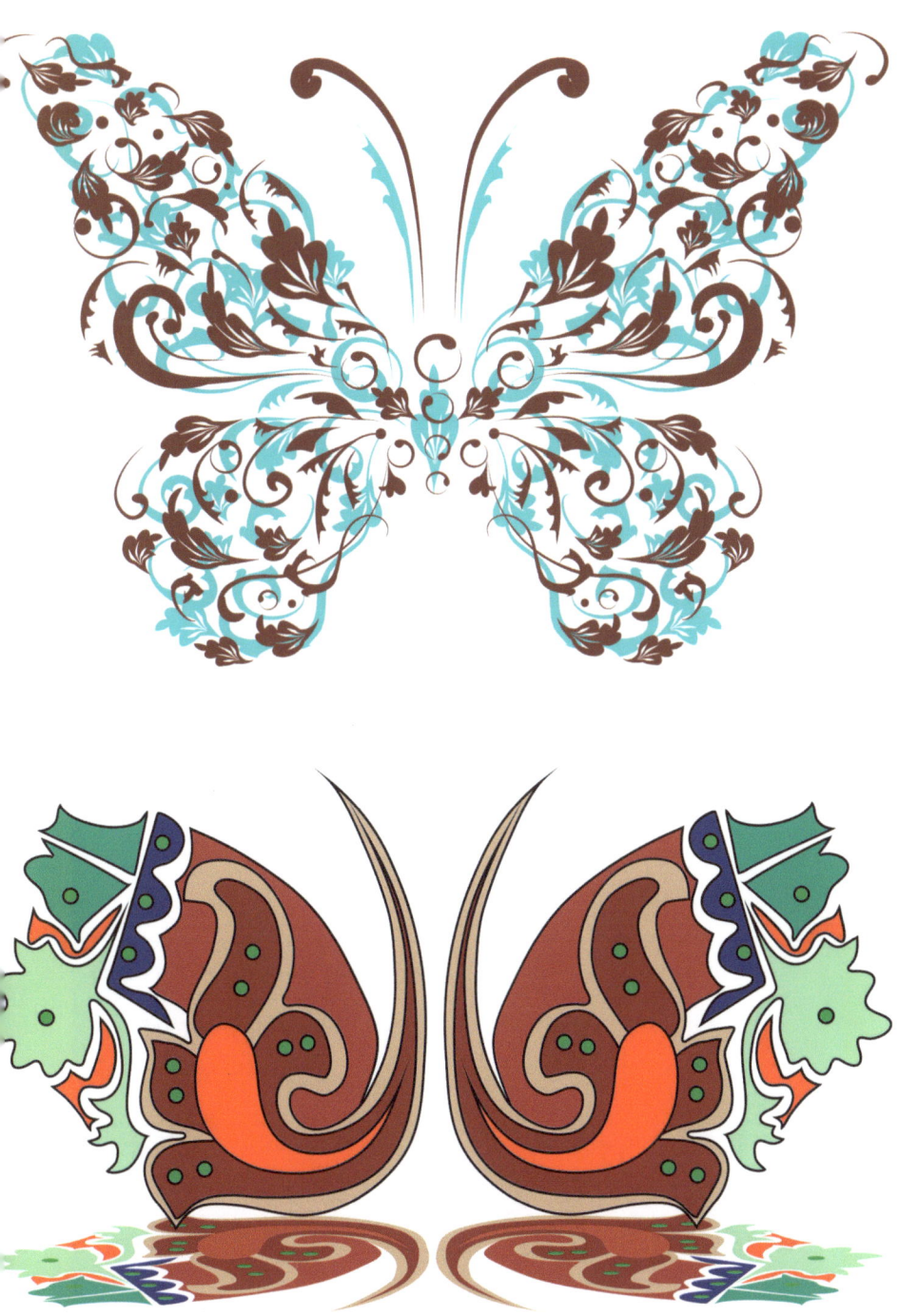

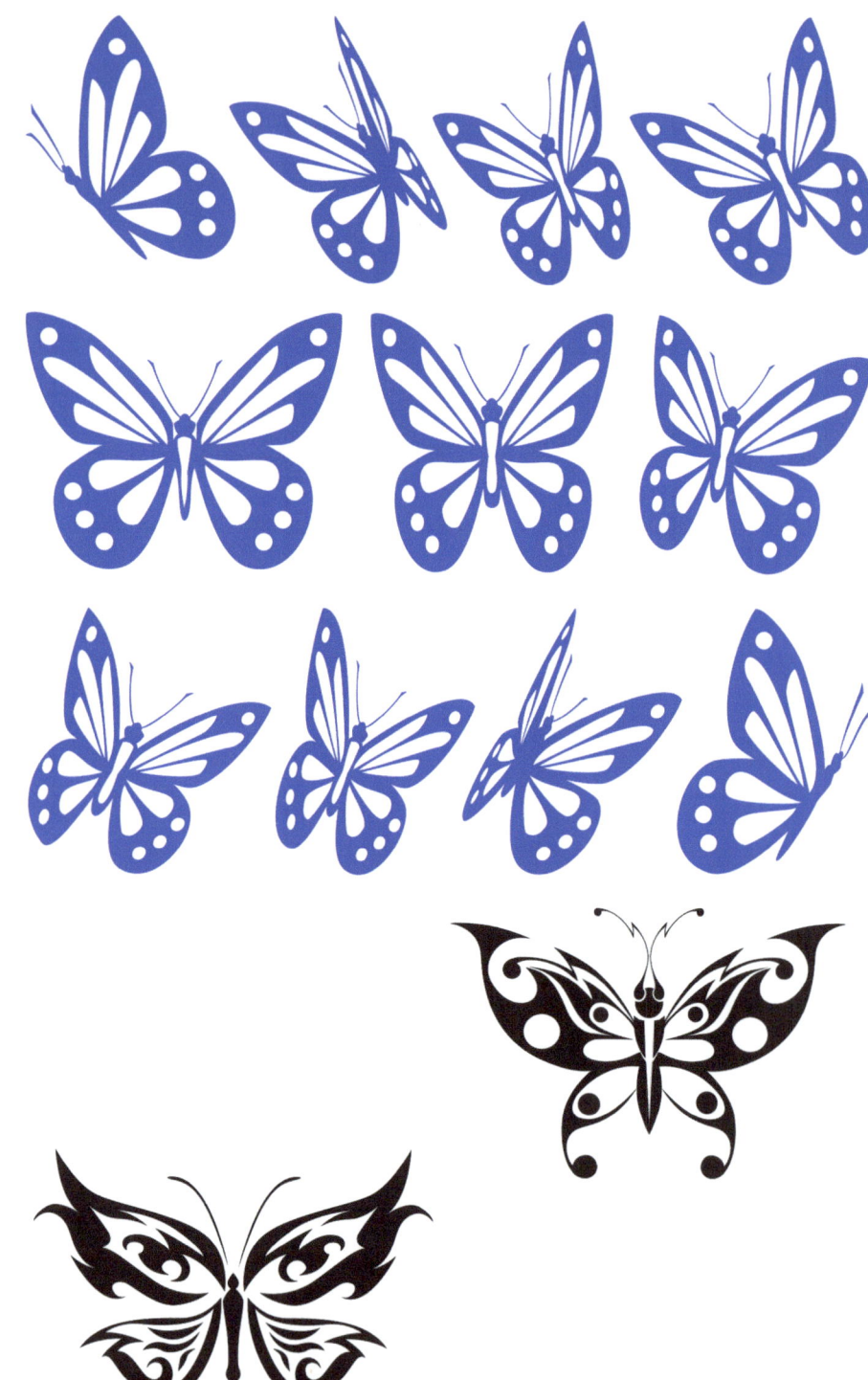

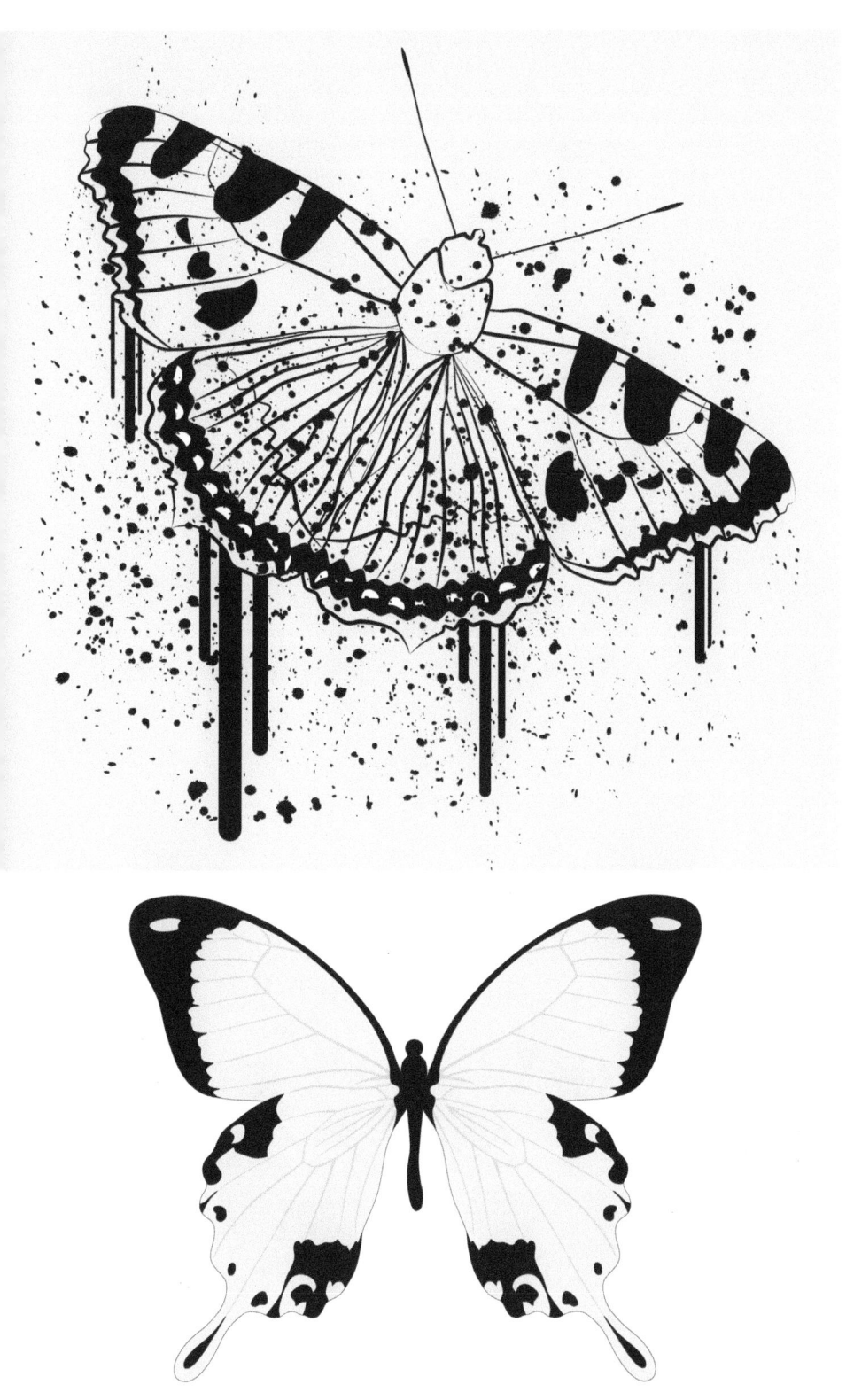

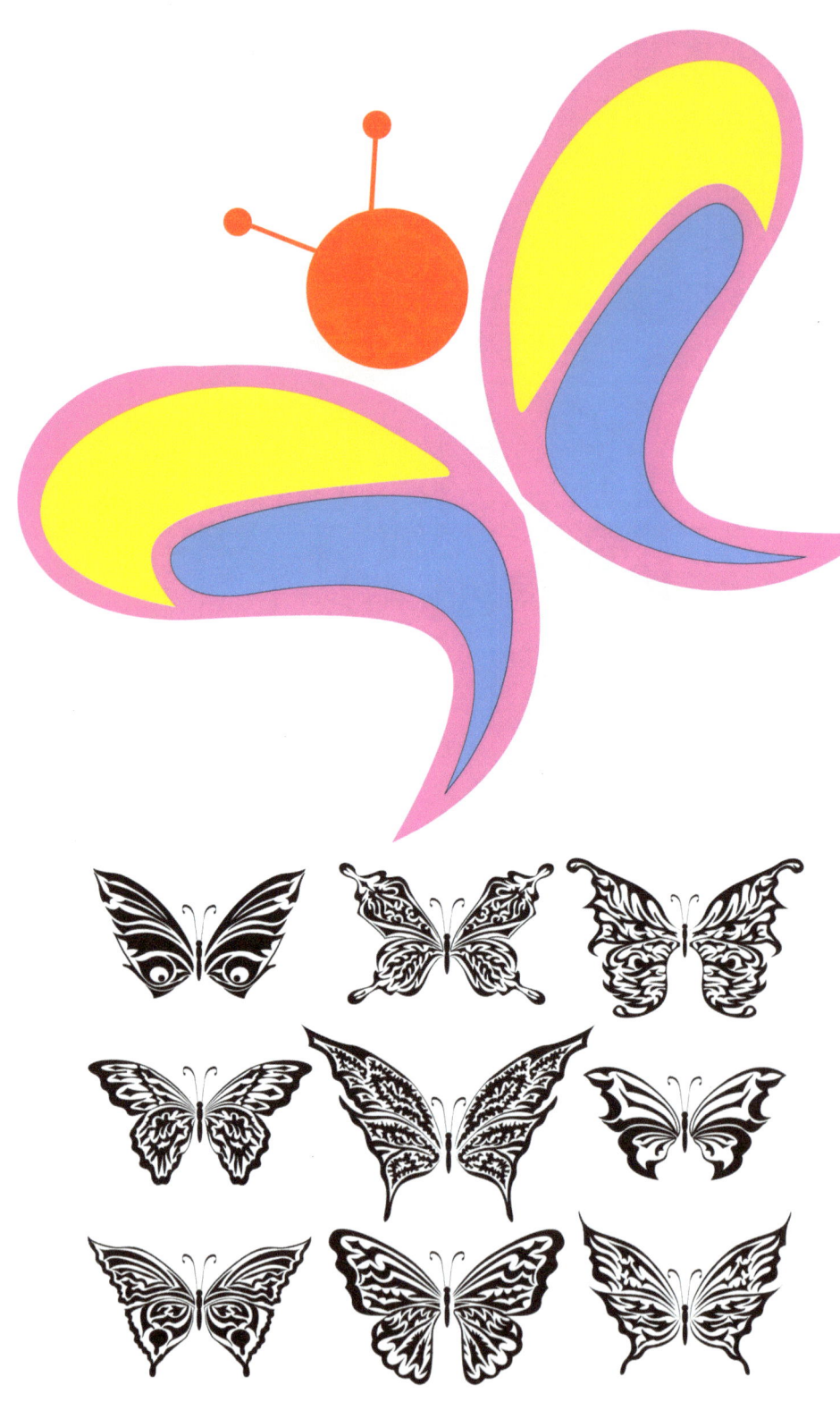

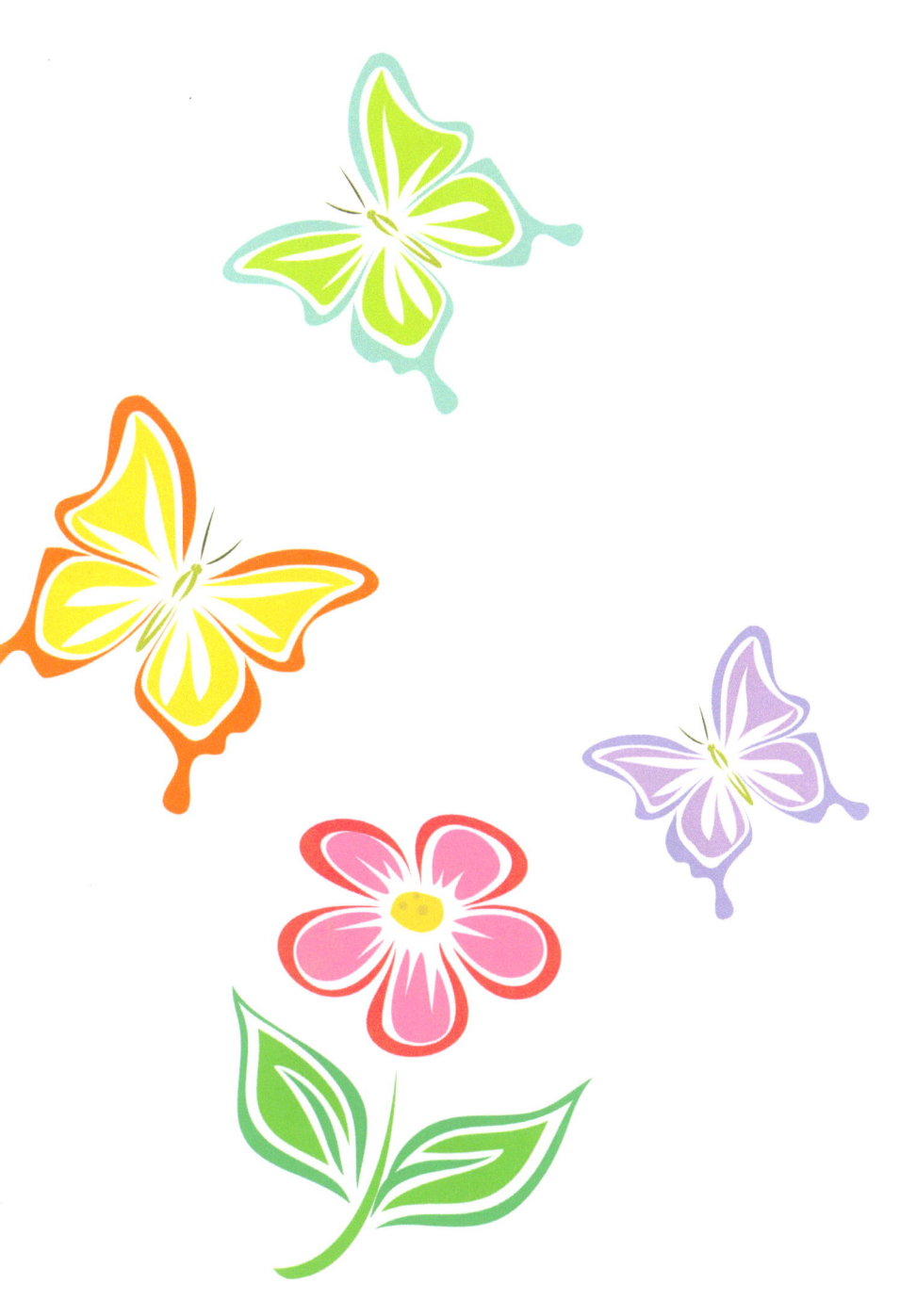

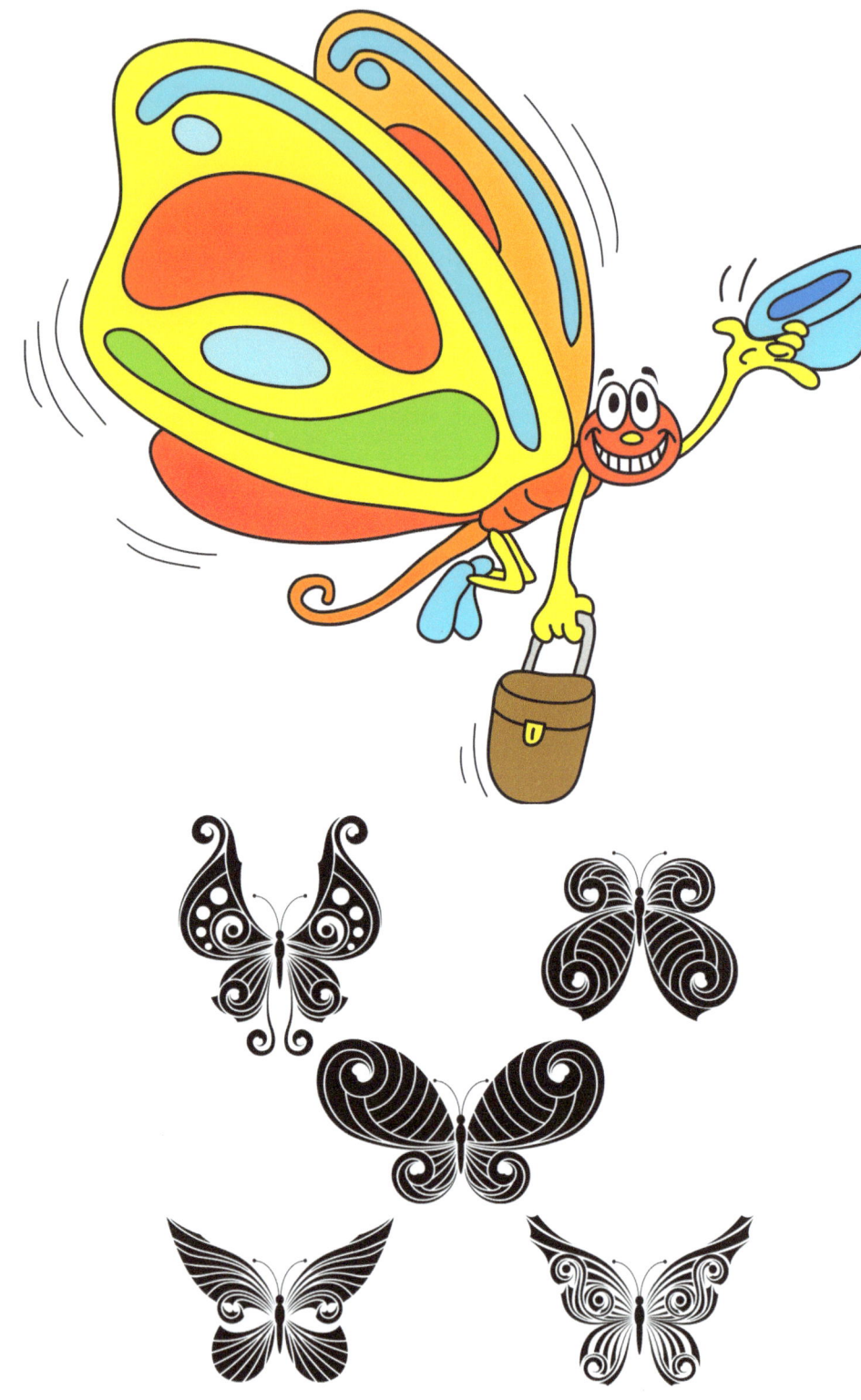

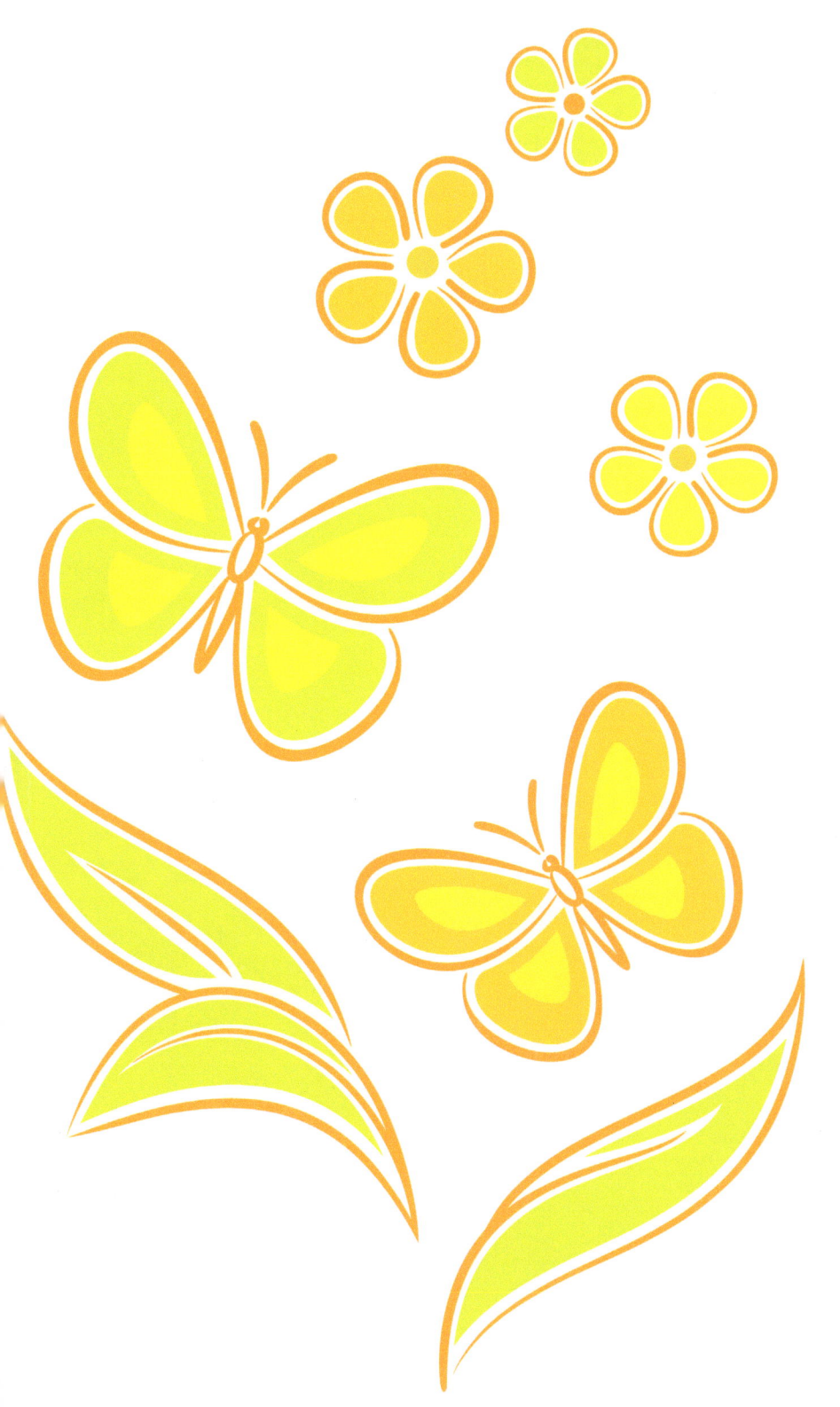

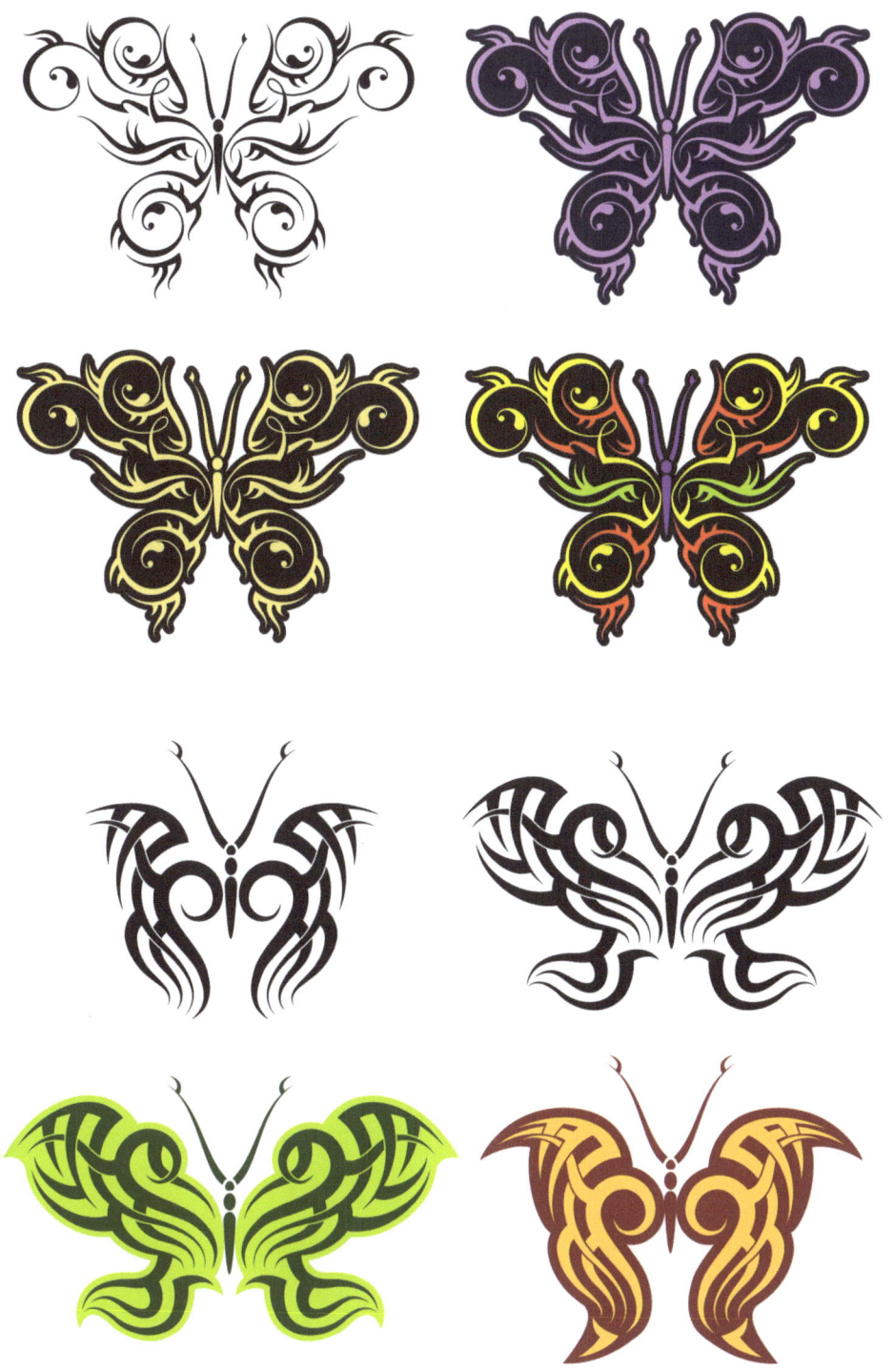

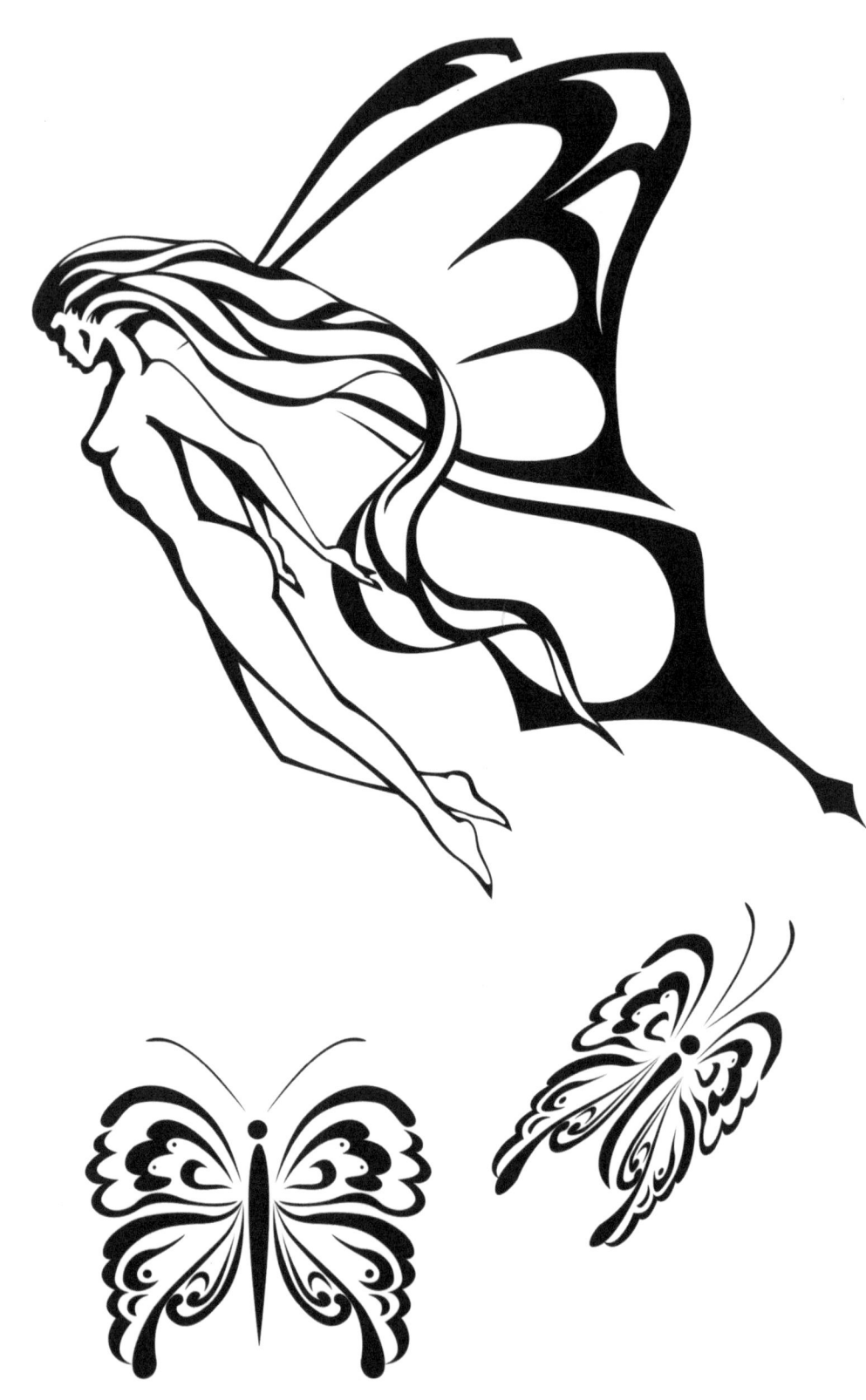

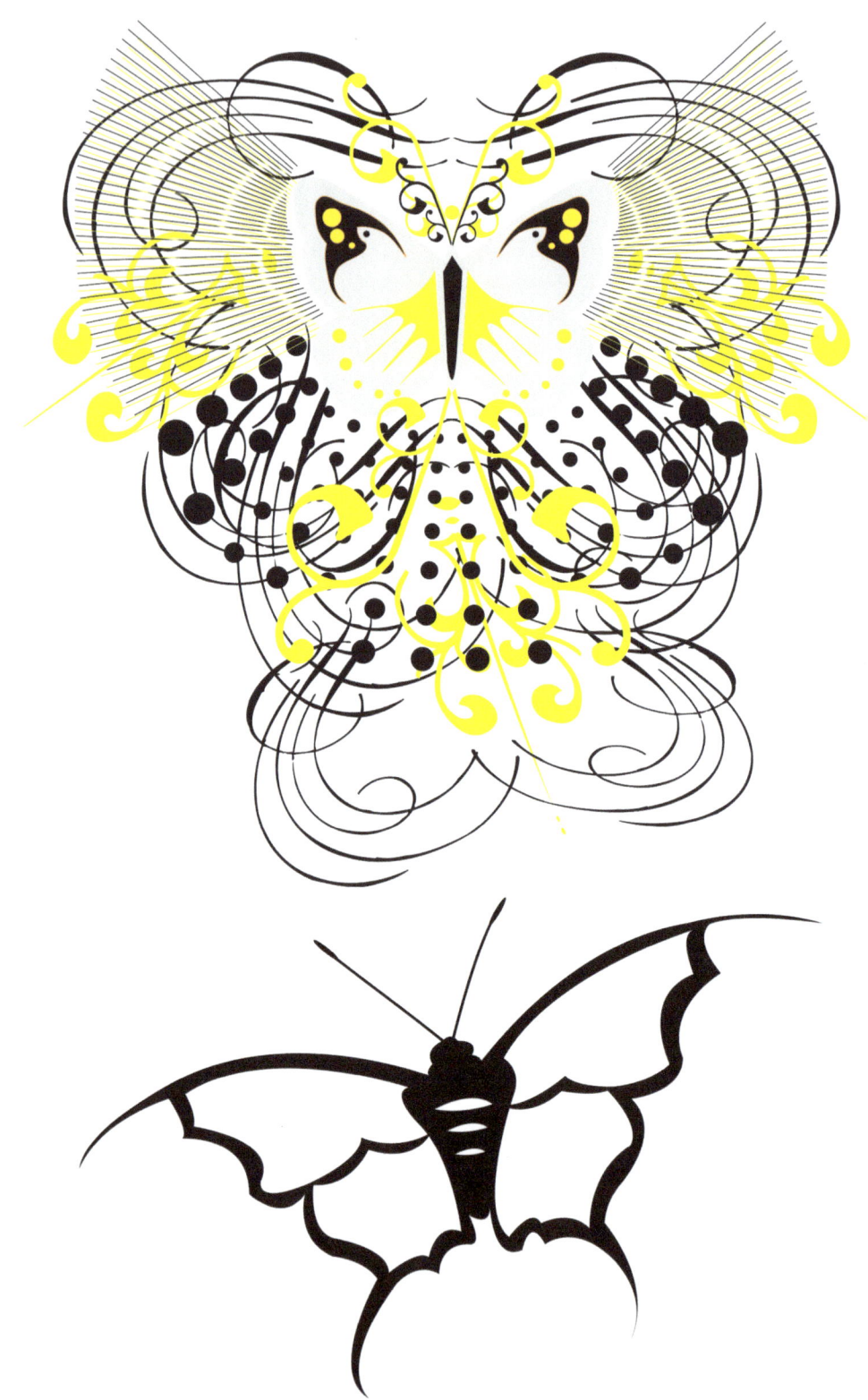

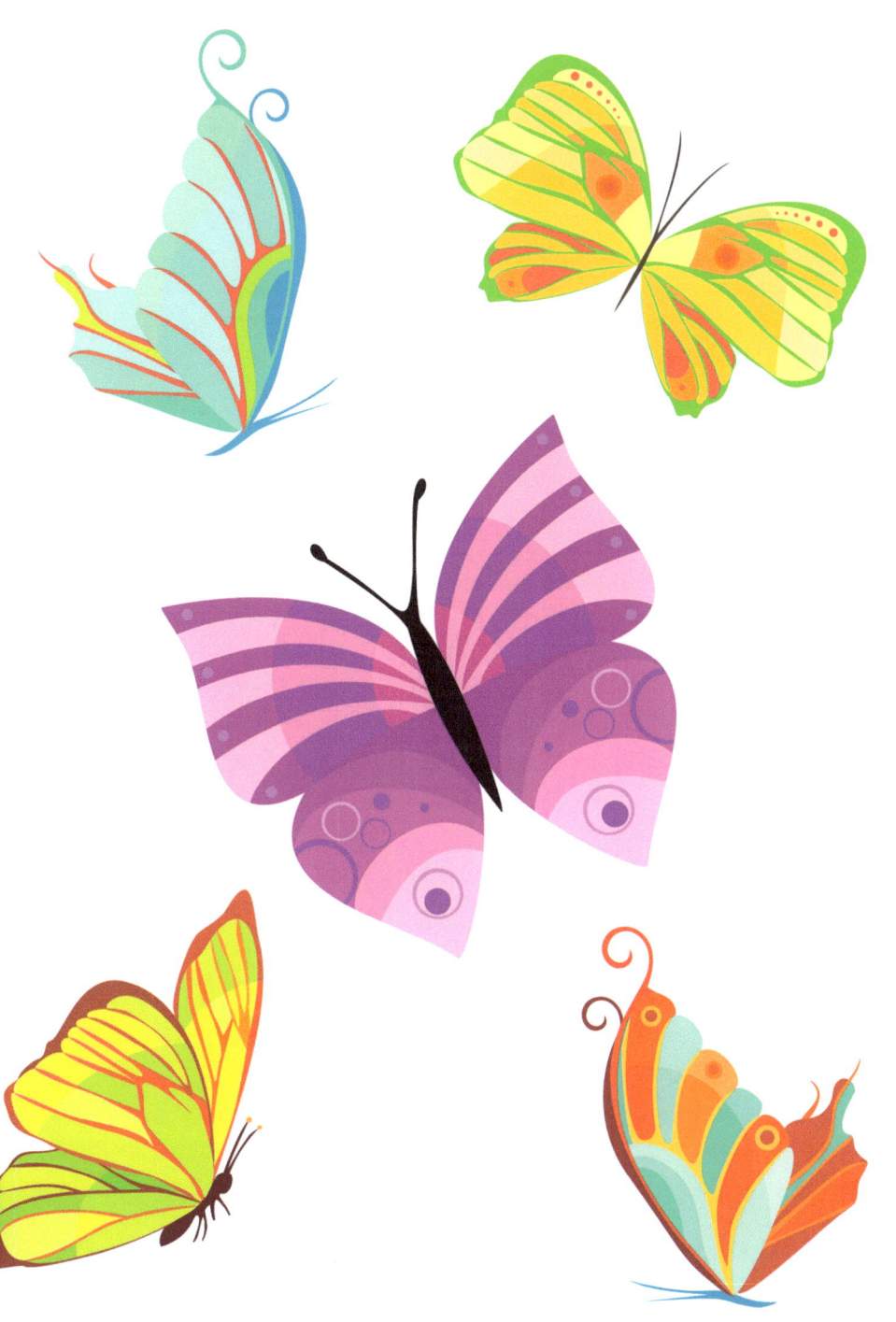

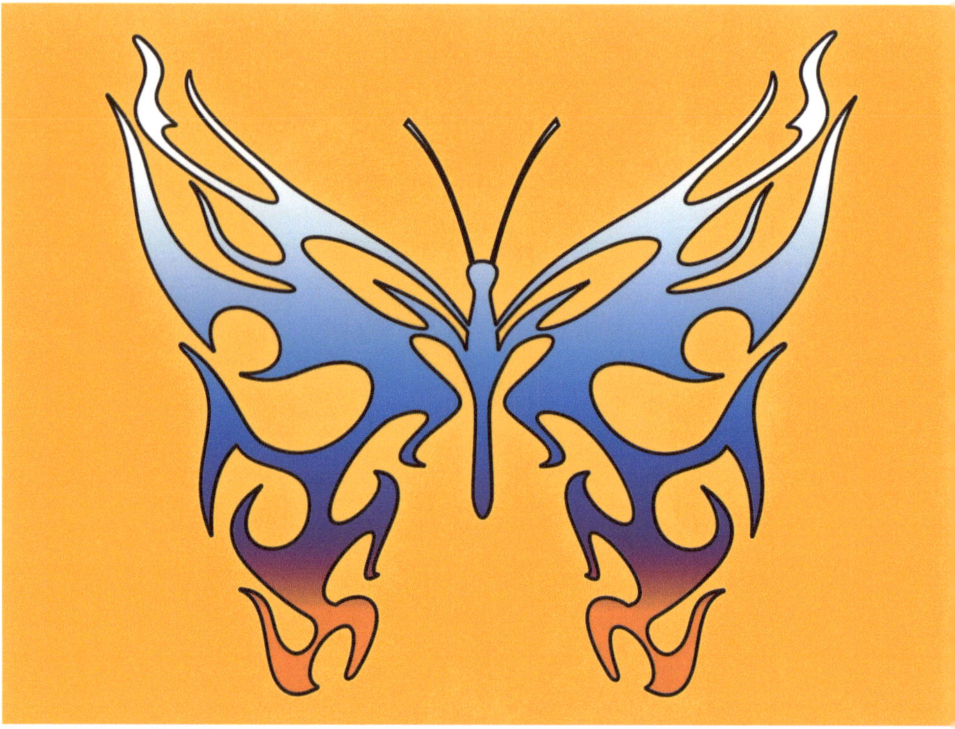

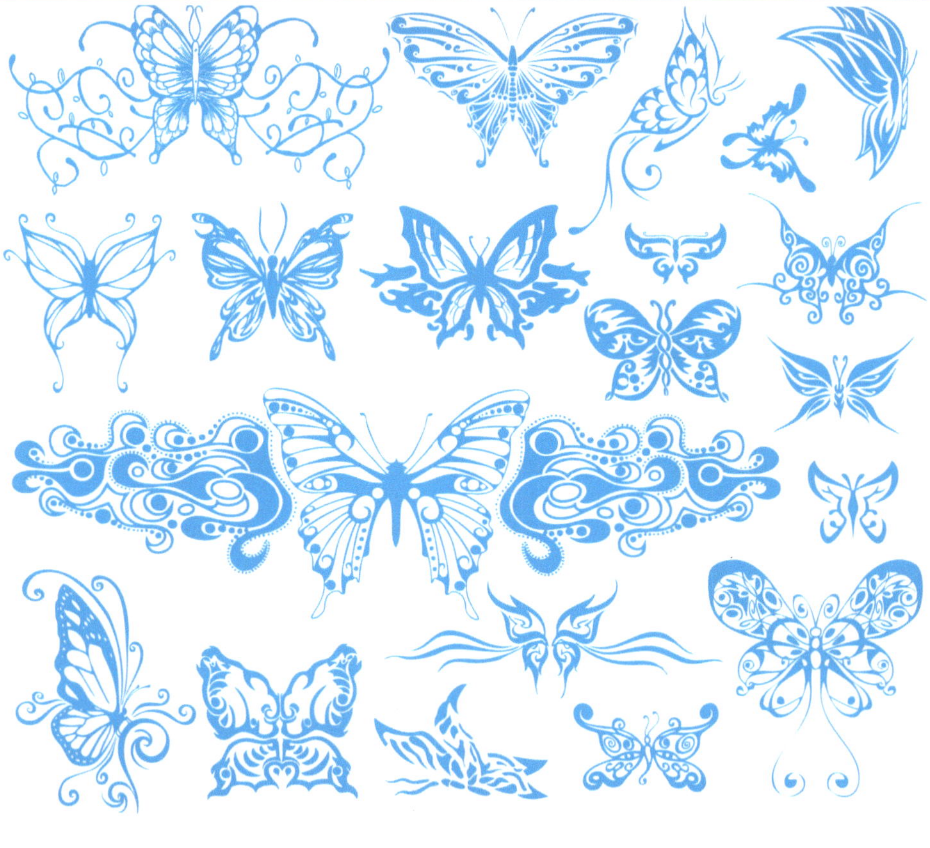

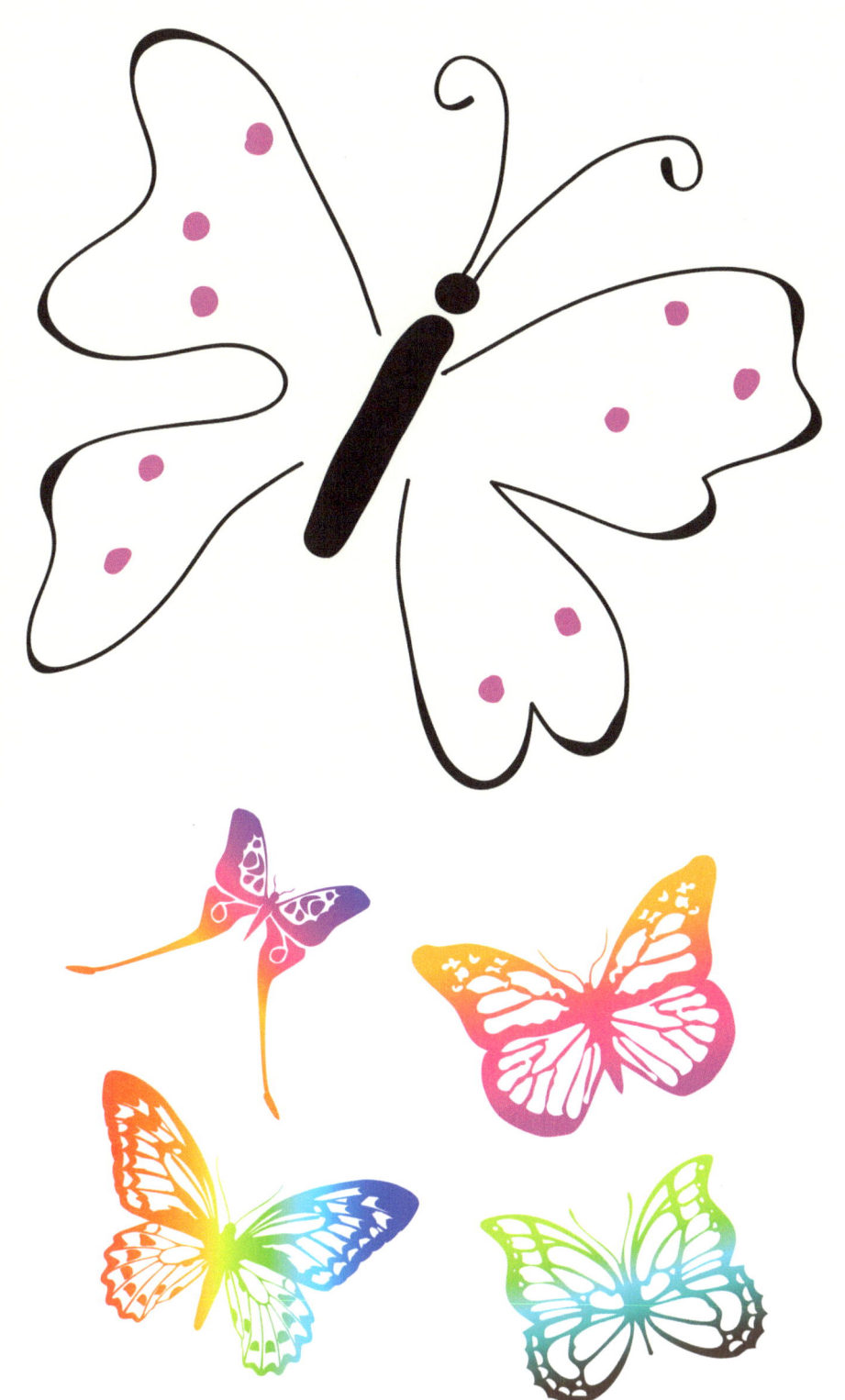

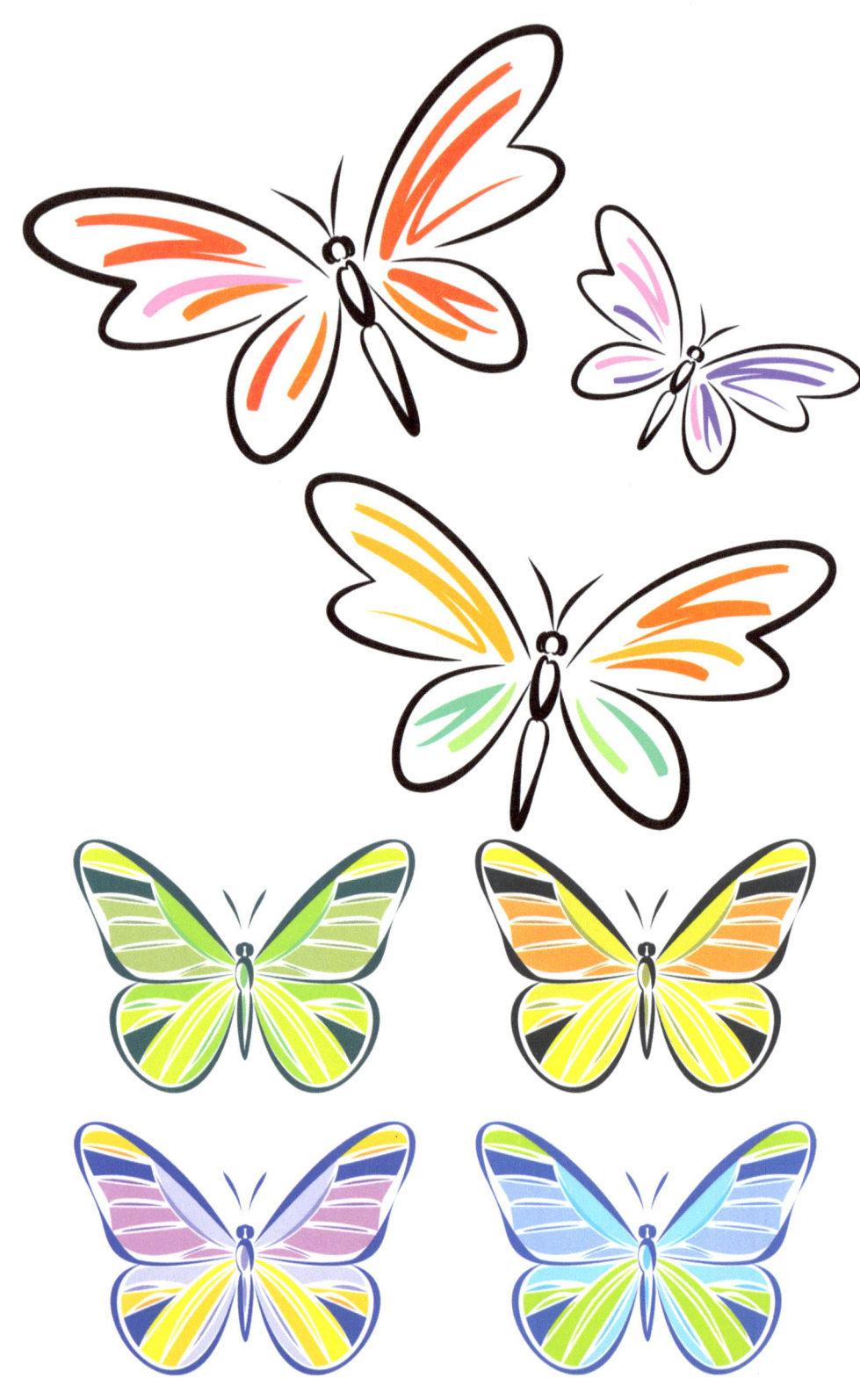

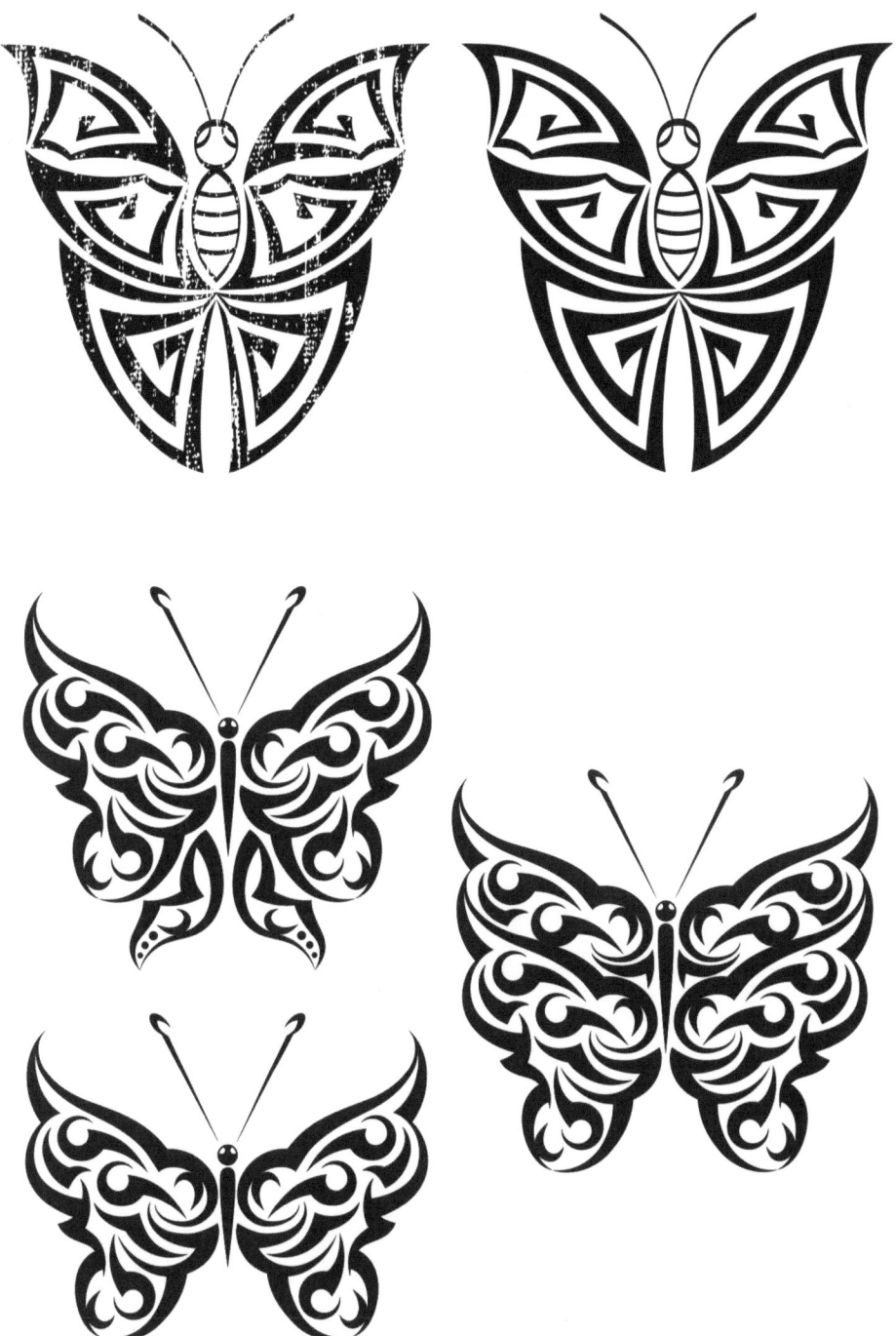

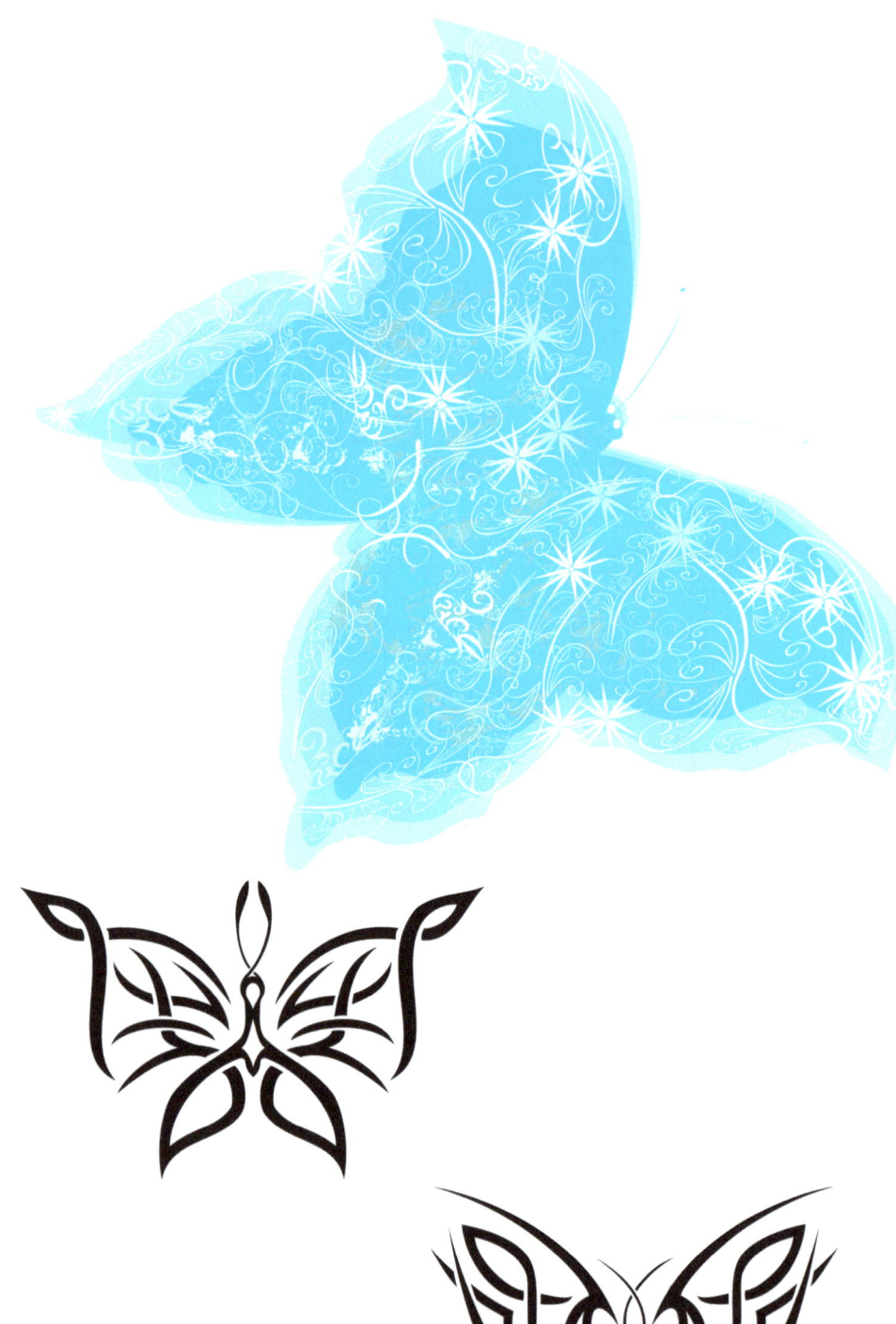

www.ingramcontent.com/pod-product-compliance
Lightning Source LLC
Chambersburg PA
CBHW040825180526
45159CB00001B/65